Jesus' Beginning

A Filipino Pastor's Powerful Encounter with God

By Joven Platilla

Giant Publishing Company
Lincoln, Nebraska, USA

2018 by Joven Platilla

Published by Giant Publishing Company
Post Office Box 6455
Lincoln, NE 68506
www.giantpublishingcompany.com

Printed in the United States of America

Jesus' Beginning – A Filipino Pastor's Powerful Encounter with God

ISBN 978-0-9995873-4-8

Non-fiction/Joven Platilla

1. Religion/Christianity
2. Christian living
3. Christian testimony

Table of contents

Jesus' beginning

John 15:5: *I am the vine, ye are the branches: He that abideth in me, and I in him, the same bringeth forth much fruit: for without me ye can do nothing.*

Life without Jesus is not worth living for. It's filled with grief, sorrow, worries and fear. It's like a dried tree with no root in the ground. Like a ship without a rudder to point it in its direction, tossed by the waves here and there. Routine, no excitement, no purpose, and no beauty - this is when we are apart from the source of life, Jesus.

I once had this kind of life. We are a product of a broken family. Our late father used to spend much of his time with his friends, drinking alcohol, gambling, and taking drugs. Our mother (Prophetess) was the one who made us survive. We were four siblings, and used to be victimized by this broken relationship of our parents, although we were just young and innocent and not that aware of the reality. Perhaps it's God's grace to protect the innocent from this kind of wrong family living, until such a time that they come up to adulthood, and their minds begin to seek an answer for every confusion that this broken life brings. In her desperation to find a way to feed us, our mother had to leave our father, and suddenly she had another man to be with, thinking that this would resolve the problem of financial struggle. She wasn't able to finish her studies. In her relationship with her second husband, she ended up having three more children, and later on she and her second husband separated. Afterwards, she happened to go abroad to work, thinking that she could raise money from abroad (Saudi Arabia), and through that money she could fix our broken family alone. I remember it was 1991 when she began to leave us to go abroad, and our grandmother was the one to take care of us. She spent almost twenty years working abroad to provide our material needs, without knowing that for all those years we missed this one very important aspect of life: the spiritual.

Train up a child (spiritually) in the way he should go, so that when he/she is old he will not depart from it. And that is the way of Jesus.

This training up in the way of righteousness is what we truly missed during those times that our mother wasn't with us. We came from a Roman Catholic religion and were being taught of their creed, "I was born a Catholic, I will die a Catholic!" But praise God, his word is much more powerful than any words in heaven, on earth, and even under the earth! So that creed was destroyed when Jesus began to step into our lives.

You didn't choose me, but I chose you…a gracious word that seemed to put an end to our miserable lives of sin. I remember, as a teenager, instead of us being in a school studying, we spent our teenage time with youngsters on the street doing things that were not appropriate for young people like us. We began smoking cigarettes (this was just for a while, maybe because God in his mercy made it taste bitter to me, since I have asthmatic lungs), drinking alcohol, gambling, and later on taking illegal drugs. These were just the result of us living a life without someone to guide us in the Lord.

I also remember when my eldest brother and I used to work at Subic Metropolitan Authority (also known as SBMA) as stevedores. Our work was to carry different kinds of baggage in sacks (rice, pellets, etc.) weighing 50 kilos each. During that time, my body was strong enough to work in that place, yet later on, God intervened and made me to be found by him in an unexpected way.

My life of sin, doing vices, having a mind full of confusion, grief, worry, and fear went on until I reached the age of twenty-four. I remember my personal encounters with the Lord; these happened many times. First, I heard him speak to me through his word, John 3:16, when I attended a children's Bible study. The Bible study leader was just a young person, yet joyfully shared to us the love of God. She led us to recite and even to pray John 3:16, and she even made me lead the group after seeing me seriously listening. Though my purpose of attending that Bible study was just to have their free one cup of juice, and one piece of bread, I ended up forgetting those things, and was captured by the wonderful peace that God gave me at that time. I truly believe and am convinced that God's word is alive! It gave me the peace of heart and mind that I really longed for during those times that our mother left us to go abroad. It's true that the preaching of the gospel is very important to people, because it is God's power to save those who believe: children, youth, and adults alike.

The second encounter that I had with the Lord was when I happened to hitch a ride on the back of a pedicab, and suddenly we were going down a bridge. I wanted to get down, but I didn't know that it wasn't the right place to do so, and the driver would not allow it. In my innocent mind, I did it myself and I jumped off the pedicab without thinking of the danger (that happened in the middle of Jones bridge at Binondo, Manila, when I was eight years old). After my feet hit the ground, I immediately rolled down on the ground (it's as if my body moved on its own) to the gutter side of the bridge. The driver had no idea of what had happened. One commuter saw the incident, and just yelled at the driver, trying to tell him that I fell down. Now I understand that if there was a truck that followed us during that time, I would have immediately been crushed by it (like what I saw in some news reports), and now I understand that there is someone behind the scene that saved me from that sure danger.

Another story of God saving me from sure death took place while we were working at Subic. We came from the outside (Olongapo) and happened to spend all night drinking alcohol and taking drugs. Afterwards, and without sleep, we went on to our work carrying bags of rice on our backs and filling up a warehouse with them, up to thirty feet high (this took place at the time when Joseph Estrada was the president of our country). Then, having a strong body and arms, although I was just a little man (5'1" in height), I would put one sack of rice (50 kilos) in both my hands and boastfully lift it up like one who lifts a barbell at a gym. Then, trying to throw it up higher on the stack, the weight of it made my body to fall back. By that time, I was on the edge of the stack, and we were about to complete the thirty-feet-high filling. Immediately I fell down from that height (twenty-five feet) and was certain that the back of my head would hit the corner of the truck below (I know it for sure since my hands both hit it). Even if I lived through that incident, there was no assurance that I could still live normally. In the middle of the air, facing a certain death below, suddenly I heard a voice that whispered in my ears, "Face down!" I was falling backwards, and then suddenly upon hearing that voice, I instantly turned to face down while I was in the air falling, and that made my hands instead of the back of my head hit the corner of the truck. It created a huge sound, and that sound made my coworkers realize that I fell down. In their fear of what had happened to me, they asked me if I was still okay, and I said, "I'm fine, and still can work." I continued on with my work that day, yet my whole being was captured by what had happened. That voice that whispered in my ears saved me. Who was it? What was it? I didn't know that time for sure. But now I know that it was the saving voice of my good Shepherd. Psalms 56:13 says: *For thou hast delivered my soul from death: wilt not thou deliver my feet from falling, that I may walk before God in the light of the living?*

Those three stories of my encounters with the Lord are still fresh in my heart and mind, for I believe the Holy Spirit put them still into my remembrance to encourage me that he is with me all the time and will never forsake me.

Seeking God in the midst of nothingness

Jonah 2:5-7: *The waters compassed me about, even to the soul: the depth closed me round about, the weeds were wrapped about my head. I went down to the bottoms of the mountains; the earth with her bars was about me forever: yet hast thou brought up my life from corruption, O LORD my God. When my soul fainted within me I remembered the LORD: and my prayer came in unto thee, into thine holy temple.*

My life was still meaningless at that time. It was a routine lifestyle; you wake up to eat your breakfast and have your coffee, then go to work, then go back home, eat your dinner, and go back to sleep to again have other day. Going to a party to drink alcohol and take drugs, or swimming at a beach, or attending occasions (birthdays and different kinds of celebrations) were just ways to make our happiness and to temporarily forget the misery of life. And this went on for years. At night, I used to look at the stars and try to behold their twinkling light, and sometimes talk to them as if they could hear me. I was looking for the meaning of life. My life was empty. I used to be happy by the things I had around me, but that was only temporary. Our mother was still in Saudi Arabia during that time, and our siblings were in Manila, and we (my eldest brother and I) were at Subic working. We had a resting place at one of the barangays at the end part of Subic; that place called "Minanga." In that place, we met people that treated us as if we were their own family, although some people there used to insult us because of our work as stevedores. Then in that place we found our second place that we called home. They welcomed us, and even showed kindness to us. I met different people, and even had different experiences in that place. Some experiences led me to once again encounter that voice that whispered in my ear while I was falling.

One time, while I was working, I was in one of the warehouses at Naval Mug, a mountainous area of Subic (I found out that the Americans used this place as their place of hiding their armory in the war against the Japanese). The voice again spoke to me and said, "What are you doing in this place? Why are you here?" I was wondering upon hearing that voice if it was just me talking to myself, or, if someone unseen was there speaking to me. I didn't know what to say in reply to that question. It went on a couple of times. This voice used to ask me, "Why are you doing such things?" etc., until my heart recognized that it was God. Then, I happened to visit a little chapel in that place and knelt down praying before the images and sculptures of what they called saints and angels. That is the way of the Roman Catholic. I prayed that time, saying, "God, if you are true/alive, show yourself to me!" That was my prayer, and that prayer was being answered by the Almighty God in process.

The knowledge of God

Acts 17:30-31: *And the times of this ignorance God winked at; but now commandeth all men everywhere to repent: Because he hath appointed a day, in the which he will judge the world in righteousness by that man whom he hath ordained; whereof he hath given assurance unto all men, in that he hath raised him from the dead.*

God is sovereign over all his creation. Yes, there is evil around us, but nevertheless God is in full control of everything. We know this passage that says in Romans 8:28: *And we know that all things work together for good to them that love God, to them who are the called according to his purpose.*

God in his mercy moved me from that place (at Subic) that time because our mother was about to go back home. I went home, my brother decided to stay at Subic, and our grandmother (who was in charge of our siblings all those years) decided to dwell at Cogeo Antipolo city with one of her sisters. I decided to go home so as to meet our mother, and to know the situations of our siblings, although I still had a plan of going back to Subic afterwards. But God didn't want me to. Almost two weeks passed by after I went home, and during that time I suffered, having asthma. I thought that time that it's just an ordinary dry cough. But it happened for two weeks, and that made my body to become weak, and I was not able to go back to work at Subic again. I don't know what was happening during that time. Although my body was weakened by the asthma, my stubborn mind still wanted to go back to Subic. Our time with our mother only lasted for two months, and then she once again went back to Saudi. Then, in my waiting for my body to come back to its composure so as to be fit for working, I happened to meet one of my friends that invited me to their Bible study in their house. I gave in, and in that Bible study I heard the good news about Jesus Christ. And somehow, I knew in my heart that I had met him many times, although I wasn't knowing him during those times. This passage in the book of Isaiah tells me, (45:5): *I am the LORD, and there is none else, there is no God beside me: I girded thee, though thou hast not known me.*

God saved me many times and was watching over me, EVEN THOUGH I DIDN'T KNOW HIM YET! Hallelujah! This knowledge of God's unfailing love fills the emptiness of my life.

In that Bible study I was asked to surrender my life to Jesus, and that I did, without hesitation. It's as if that was God's appointed time for me so that I had nothing to say but, "Yes, Lord!" We read in the four gospels when Jesus called his twelve disciples to be his followers, and they responded without a thought. Truly God has an appointed time for everything, even for salvation.

So, this voice that saved me, that guided me, that even helped me, is Jesus Christ. That moment that I entrusted my life to him, at that Bible study when I decided to follow him, even though I didn't know what it really meant to follow him, my heart and mind were filled with wonderful peace that made me speechless for an hour. It was as if I was floating into an ecstasy. All my worries, my fears, and the longing deep within me were being filled by him at that time.

The friend that invited me to his house to attend that Bible study is none other than Brother Daniel. And he is now one of our associate pastors in the church. I found out later that he is an evangelist. Some of our leaders in the church were evangelized by him. Truly God will appoint a time, an event, and even a person to each of us so as to save us. That day is predestined before the foundation of the world. I also now understand that faith is one of the important parts for that saving day of Jesus to be discovered by us. Faith can be working through prayer, inviting people to Bible study/church, preaching, even by setting an example of the life of a true believer of Christ before them (unbelievers). In this, many used to doubt our Christian faith, because many used to live contrary to the message of the gospel.

Born again

John 3:3: *Jesus answered and said unto him, Verily, verily, I say unto thee, Except a man be born again, he cannot see the kingdom of God.*

1 Peter 1:23: *Being born again, not of corruptible seed, but of incorruptible, by the word of God, which liveth and abideth for ever.*

I used to hear and see people that are in this faith, and even tried to mock them due to my ignorance, without knowing that one day I would be one of them. Praise God that I'm one of them now - me and my household. This life as a follower of Jesus is what occupies my life as an adult. I forgot working again at Subic (although I had my thought of returning there, not to become a stevedore again, but to preach to them the gospel). My new life in Jesus began and went on as I attended fellowships. Brother Daniel patiently assisted me during those times. I believe God was using him to help me until I grew up in this faith. Before I became a believer, I was a sinner (all of us are, of course), and I used to be in a wrong relationship. I fell in love with the cousin of my mother, and our relationship began from the time that I went home to Antipolo, and then continued on even until I became a Christian. At first, I was just curious about it. I also was being motivated by anger toward our grandmother. I thought that in this way I could retaliate against her for her harsh treatment of us. Because of that we became rebellious. Our grandmother learned such harsh treatment toward her children from her mother, and we also observed that it was passed on to generations.

As a believer, I now was struggling with this lust that put me in bondage. Even after I attended a fellowship to know more of this new life in Christ, sin used to be closer to me at this time than before. It was more real and seemed to really want to pull me down. I prayed that God would remove this from me, since I never wanted to be in this life of a sinner again. I remember when this girl and I used to be on a date, and doing the things that we were not supposed to do, I heard this voice in my ear that said, "Shame on you!" The voice was clear, as if someone approached me and told me this in my ear. I was thinking who it was, and later found out that it was Satan, the accuser of the brethren. He tempted me, and I gave in, and now he wanted me to feel condemned. I suffered much from that voice of condemnation from Satan, to the point of being discouraged to continue attending a fellowship. But God's grace is greater than my weakness. We know that apostle Paul used to have weaknesses, as a thorn in the flesh, an instrument of Satan to humiliate him, and he asked God to remove it, but God's answer comforted the heart and mind of the apostle by saying, *My grace is sufficient for you. My strength is made perfect in weakness.* (2 Corinthians 12:9). God didn't remove the struggle of Paul, but what he did seemed to give us a profound knowledge of our loving God on how he deals with sin. He empowered the apostle and thereby gave him the ability to overcome his weaknesses.

For months, as a believer, I still managed to drink alcohol because of the temptation made by Satan through my friends. And even my wrong relationship toward that girl still happened, until such a time that I cried out to God, and humbly asked him to find a way that I may be able to escape from this temptation that I thought was stronger than I. During that time, I used to read the Bible, and for months managed to finish it from cover to cover. But we also know that the more we draw near to God, Satan is also present, wanting to distract us.

Paul in his letter to the Romans said (7:15): *For that which I do I allow not: for what I would, that do I not; but what I hate, that do*

I. And also, in verses19-23: *For the good that I would I do not: but the evil which I would not, that I do. Now if I do that I would not, it is no more I that do it, but sin that dwelleth in me. I find then a law, that, when I would do good, evil is present with me. For I delight in the law of God after the inward man: But I see another law in my members, warring against the law of my mind, and bringing me into captivity to the law of sin which is in my members.*

And he cried out in Romans 7:24: *O wretched man that I am! Who shall deliver me from the body of this death?*

Sinners are hopeless; doomed to die in sin, and they will go to hell after. Good works, intellectual ideas, money, fame, etc., can't make us get out of this hopeless life! One of the most foolish thoughts that mankind did in order to deny this truth of man's hopelessness is to not believe the existence of God. And these people we call atheists. To them, using their corrupted heart and mind, with the physical knowledge (theories and observations) that they have, they try to remove God from His existence. To them, if there is no God, then there should be no law, no sin, and no punishment. This is the biggest lie ever made by Satan that was entertained by his slaves. However, to us, we know and believe that God exists! Romans 11:36: *For of him, and through him, and to him, are all things: to whom be glory for ever. Amen.*

Sin seemed like a huge wall that used to stop me and separated me from Christ (Isaiah 59:2), and I was desperately seeking a way to destroy that wall, and found out that those efforts were futile. Men's efforts to destroy sin are powerless; there is only one power that can destroy sin, and that is the power of God. Jesus is the power of God to destroy sin. He first showed that power from the Old Testament, and it was finished on a cross! Yes, on a cross Christ's final victory over sin was finished, and the power of his finished work on a cross was distributed toward his people.

Going back to that wrong relationship, I pled to God earnestly to make a way for me, for I couldn't do it on my own. Then he made a way by making us to move to another place: from Antipolo, we transferred to Laguna (Los Banos). My elder sister visited us, and invited us to be in their place, and this was agreed to by us, and we live at Laguna even now (2006 up to present).

This made me to escape from the snare of Satan, although I still managed to meet that girl, but that was only to end our relationship. It wasn't easy; emotionally I was broken. But God is there to help us through. I remember the day when that girl and I parted our ways, I went home and felt the brokenness. I was listening to a song that has to do with a broken relationship and this song made me to feel the pain strongly. Then suddenly God whispered to me and said, "Why not listen to my song for you?" and he moved me to listen to a gospel song entitled, "One Way Jesus". This was being popularized by Hillsong in Australia. I remember listening to that song. That time it was just through a tape, and each and every lyric/message of that song really sank into every detail of my spirit. The song is a praise song; it's sung fast. But when I was listening to it, it was as if the song was played slowly into my ear, that I could almost see and understand its message. The song led me to the part that says, "You were always, always there, every how and everywhere. Your grace abounds so deeply within me!" The Lord moved me to realize that he was with me, and used to guide and watch over me even when I hadn't known him yet. That even after I surrendered my life to him, and even though I again got involved with the wrong things: he still was there! And he was there watching me doing these things that hurt him. He was there even trying to find a way for me to escape from these things, though sadly often I gave in to the temptation rather than to run away from it. He was there watching me trying to survive, to get out of that muddy place of sin, for he knows in my heart that I belong to him. He was there to even lessen the consequences of the mistakes that I made, for if he didn't, I would not be here telling you this story as a servant of God. I know now, that if God wouldn't help me get out of that place of sin, and put a stop to this fire of hell that used to consume me little by little, that I would end up being burned spiritually, and that my life would again become messy. Praise God that he was and is always, always there! As he promised, "I will never leave you nor forsake you!"

Walking with the Lord

Here in Laguna we (our family, and also brother Daniel) came to settle, and to look for a job at Robinson's Mall. We, brother Daniel, I, and my brother applied for a job there. (Although it's forbidden for siblings to work there in the same branch or company, we managed to do some falsifications in order to be accepted by them: I changed my name, and used the name of one of my brothers that had a different surname (from his father)). To make a long story short, Daniel and I were hired as janitors, and to my surprise my eldest brother wasn't hired. Then, I also remember that we were looking for a Christian church here the first time, and were praying to God to lead us into the right place of fellowship. We happened to meet one of the pastors from my former church, in which we were told of different kinds of Christian fellowships, and then we ended up attending the church in which he was one of the associate pastors. We faithfully attended that church for years, and were able to participate in their activities. Daniel and I got involved with the youth ministry for a time, and I ended up resigning my work and decided to be one of the youth leaders. For all those times, we little by little invited our family into the church, even one by one. The last member that we made to be a believer, and that is by the grace of God, was our grandmother, who used to be our persecutor before. Truly God's promise in Acts 16:31 is powerful.

God led me to know him more in his word, and he gave me this hunger and thirst for his word, that as a new believer I managed to read his word (with taking notes) for a time of at least one to two hours. To a new believer, it's just like a baby drinking one gallon of milk a day! Even after having that spiritual walk with the Lord, God also led me to even read some spiritual books. Not all of the Christian books are spiritual books, but as a new believer I didn't have the knowledge and wisdom to identify which ones were spiritual and which ones were just a theory, or just a man's point of view (even if they backed it up with scriptures). God in his supernatural way (some by other believers' testimonies, some by the Lord's prompting) led me to read books that he used to guide me. My life during those years used to be: read the Bible, read spiritual books (yet the Bible is the best), attend a fellowship (Bible study, prayer meeting, Sunday worship, seminars, etc.) and nothing was there to stop me from doing so. My eldest brother and I worked together to bring our family to Christ, and to let them serve him also. Our mother found out that we got involved with the Christian fellowship and was happy, thinking that it would be good for us to be there rather than to be with the friends that lead us to do evil things, yet in her mind she wasn't yet convicted by the Lord. When the time came that I decided to go into full-time ministry, she didn't agree with me. She thought that I didn't have to that, for she was listening to her doubtful mind then.

The Lord used to amaze me by the knowledge and revelations that I received from him (through the Bible meditation and the other books). I read the testimony of Mary K. Baxter (*A Divine Revelation of Heaven; A Divine Revelation of Hell*), *The Purpose Driven Life* by Rick Warren, and so on. He also had me read spiritual warfare books -books that give us the knowledge of casting out demons, speaking in tongues, spiritual gifts and power, etc. While I was doing my personal research of Christian doctrines, I also managed to listen to different preachers (with different perspectives of the Bible). I happened to come to the point of asking myself whether my understanding of the scriptures is true and accurate, or not? Upon hearing preachers preaching a different point of view of the Bible, I later found out by God's help that it was just their own point of view and not the real teaching of the Holy Spirit (remember that the Holy Spirit will lead us into all truth (of God's word and power) John 14:26, 16:13). Many were misled   and   were   corrupted   later   on   by   these   false teachers/preachers that are inside the church. This happened because of many factors: lack of personal meditation on God's word, lack of prayer, lack of discernment, idolizing men, etc. I was confused then, and puzzled about how I might be able to confirm whether I was not being misled by my own personal study and by others' messages. By then the Holy Spirit led me to go into the Bible school. Don't get me wrong, please, the Holy Spirit is our guide into all truth, but for me, he had to bring me into the Bible school for me to study the formal and in-depth methods of interpretations. I wasn't able to finish my high school study while I was a teenager, due to the lack of support (morally and financially) at that time, and the Bible school required us to present our high school diploma, because it is a college school. This thought of having a high school diploma didn't worry me; I was determined to find a way to go into the Bible school no matter what it took. I was just in a first-year high school before and wasn't able to finish it, so I had to study again for four years in high school so as to have a diploma (I was already twenty-four years old, and I didn't care!). I remember when the pastor (he is now a bishop) of my former church asked me when we were in his office, "Joven, please tell me, what is your plan for your life now?"

And I told him without hesitation, "Pastor, I want to go to the Bible school."

Then he said, "Okay, that's fine. Let's go and made an inquiry." To make a long story short, instead of studying four more years in high school, I had to do just one year with the "Out of School Adult (OSA)program. It is now called ALS (Alternative Learning System). This program is to help adults continue their study, even after stopping it for a long time. We were told that if we were able to pass the acceleration exam that they would give us at the month of the school year, we could then immediately have our high school diplomas. It seemed a way of a short cut. I praised God that I didn't have to stay with the youngsters for four years in a high school. We were almost fifty students, and many used to be intellectual, others were already on the second- and third-year level, and by the grace of God, I alone managed to pass the test in that group! So, I took my diploma and got enrolled into the Bible school. At this time, my former pastor discouraged me to go into a Bible school, for so many reasons, but nevertheless, I pursued my heart's desire, even after knowing that my pastor was not going to support me (and even the church would not!). One of the associate pastors helped me get into that Bible school; praise God for his life. And I was there in the Bible school for all those years, and God led me to become passionate in my study. Not all Bible school students are that serious in their study, and even in our group, only a few managed to finish their study for different reasons, and of those that graduated (we were seven) only four of us went on into the full-time ministry. I cherished my life in school, even though during that time I happened to get involved with things that used to make me neglect my study. Truly Satan has many ways to distract us from following Jesus, but God is faithful to establish us every time we decide to serve him.

Temptations everywhere

James 1:13-16: *Let no man say when he is tempted, I am tempted of God: for God cannot be tempted with evil, neither tempteth he any man: But every man is tempted, when he is drawn away of his own lust, and enticed. Then when lust hath conceived, it bringeth forth sin: and sin, when it is finished, bringeth forth death. Do not err, my beloved brethren.*

You may think that places like a church, Bible school, etc., can be a safe place from Satan's temptation or demonic works. But you are wrong in that! Satan can send demons all over the world so as to do his evil works, even if it is in your church, or in the Bible school. In the school some students, including myself, got involved with watching pornographic movies, and even flirting in chat (messaging or video). In the school, you may decide to spend your time studying the Bible, and some books, or spend it in satisfying your sinful nature. I heard many students and even professors got involved in these evil works, but praise God that the Holy Spirit is there to convict us of our sin. God rebuked me gently for doing these filthy things (by that time, our mother had given me a lap top computer as a gift). I stopped watching pornography, and even tried to stop others by doing it. I was the maintenance man of the computer room, so I made it a rule to forbid everyone to open a porno movie, for these movies often had viruses in them. The problem is that, you may stop the student, but you can't do it that easily to the professors and some pastors that used to study there. Some managed to continue to watch those bad movies, and I had no knowledge as to how I might recognize it in a computer (such as to know the history of browsing), until such a time that the computer in a room we were using was crashed by a virus that came from a pornographic website. This made the administrator get angry with us (he has been a Korean missionary here in the Philippines for more than twenty years), and he was surprised by this evil thing. Of course, no one admitted that sin, and this resulted in the removal of the computer from that room. What a tragic event. See, the thief comes only to steal, kill and destroy! And he destroyed not just our computer there, but also our dignity as students of God's word. But praise God that he always forgives us every time we confess our sins, and gives us so many chances to serve him, though as a part of learning he allowed us to suffer a little consequence of our mistakes. Even after that temptation of pornographic movies, one came after another. Like Pharaoh that pursued Israel into the wilderness, trying to enslave them again, Satan used to pursue me into that place, trying to stop me from doing the will of God. Again, I got involved with a wrong thing: having a relationship with my classmate (it was wrong simply because I was not really in love with her; it was just a kind of flirting relationship).

Another mistake - a networking business

1 Timothy 6:6-10: *But godliness with contentment is great gain. For we brought nothing into this world, and it is certain we can carry nothing out.   And having food and raiment let us be therewith content.   But they that will be rich fall into temptation and a snare, and into many foolish and hurtful lusts, which drown men in destruction and perdition. For the love of money is the root of all evil: which while some coveted after, they have erred from the faith, and pierced themselves through with many sorrows.*

Due to worrying for our basic needs, I tried to make money by going into a networking business as a part-time job, while I was studying in the Bible school. This networking business promised to make us rich, even in a short time. This enticed us by thinking we could put an end to our financial struggle in just a short time, and not have to return to it again. Many, even pastors (wanting to be rich instantly), were doing this. It was not illegal, although there was some scam business that deceived many at that time. The one that I went into was a good one. But, the problem with that networking business is that it will entice you to pursue money and forget your calling as a pastor, and this almost happened to me! Many used to fall into this trap - pursuing money, forgetting the church, and trying to get even the entire church membership to get involved. This ends up in trouble, with some congregations being divided, and some members getting into debt (some sell their possessions such as a lot, a house, etc., just to believe in this lie of the enemy of becoming rich instantly!). Jesus once taught us that we can't serve two masters: we can't serve God and money at the same time. To a minister like me, this is true. Yes, not all are called to be a pastor or to be in a full-time ministry of preaching and teaching the word of God. There are some members that have a calling to go on into a business in order to bless the church in terms of money and materials, but not all! I'm not saying that all networking businesses are evil. What I say is, if you are called to be a full-time minister of the word of God, don't go fall into it, but if your call is in the business ministry, then go into this networking. Yet, be cautious of the desire of wanting to be rich materially; this is the great trap of Satan to all of those that are now serving him (Matthew 4:8-9). Little by little, I ended up spending much of my time in this part-time business, and became negligent of my study in the Bible school, and I wasn't that fully aware of it since my mind was focused on looking for people that I may recruit to become my down lines in my network. I was deceived to the point of throwing away my precious pearl (time to study God's word) in exchange for a fancy beauty of money! Yet, God's mercy reached to me from heaven, and he rebuked me gently, and even warned me of losing him if I would not stop doing the business. I heard him say to me, "Who told you to do such a thing? That is Satan's trap and you fell into it. It happened simply because you didn't consult me! Now, leave it, and lay it down at my feet, and do the things you did at first."

By the grace and mercies of God, I gave up this networking business (although I had the potential to enlarge my network), and decided to go on again into my full-time study in the Bible school. During that time, I had rarely attended my classes, and mostly I was in the business company looking for people to recruit on the outside, and even tried to recruit some of my classmates and professors. God had also tried to correct me by my administrator, who advised me to stop the networking and just pursue my study, for I was called to be a minister and not a businessman. I resisted many times, since often we listen to our mind and not to the conviction given by the Holy Spirit, and this is to our hurt. Yet, still if our desire is to serve God, he will gently correct us and lead us into his way of wisdom.

Meeting my wife

Genesis 24:62-67: *Now Isaac had returned from Beer-lahai-roi and was dwelling in the Negeb. And Isaac went out to meditate in the field toward evening. And he lifted up his eyes and saw, and behold, there were camels coming. And Rebekah lifted up her eyes, and when she saw Isaac, she dismounted from the camel and said to the servant, "Who is that man, walking in the field to meet us?" The servant said, "It is my master." So she took her veil and covered herself. And the servant told Isaac all the things that he had done. Then Isaac brought her into the tent of Sarah his mother and took Rebekah, and she became his wife, and he loved her. So Isaac was comforted after his mother's death.*

I believe in God about his perfect plan for husband and wife, that there is a right partner for each, and man and woman are to meet in God's perfect time and way. As I heard from one of the prophecies given by the Lord to one of his servants, "The man/woman that I designed to be a perfect partner for each must be met by each other in my appointed time. Sometimes, time is not what matters; what matters is that you will meet each other." Our first meeting of my wife April and I wasn't planned by us; it happened unexpectedly in time. I happened to be busy at that time looking for people which I could recruit to be my down line on my networking business. At that time, I had disregarded looking for a relationship, although I was already twenty-eight years old. My mind was being caught up with the desire to be rich. Then suddenly, I happened to visit Robinson's Town Mall in Los Banos for the networking business. Suddenly, when I happened to be standing by at the place in which there was a video store, and people were there, even women, I happened to see this beautiful and lovely woman that caught my eye. When I saw her, my heart immediately beat for her, and I had somehow this feeling of wanting to know her. I gathered all my strength to approach her to ask her name, and she responded with a smile telling me, "I'm April". Her smile and beauty caught my heart, and I told myself, surely this woman is for me. We began our friendship, and in just a little time we agreed to marry each other, and now she is with me helping me to carry the cross that God made us to carry in this ministry. I praise God that he didn't allow me to fall into a relationship with another woman that would make me to go away from him. That is why it is very important that the husband or wife that you will be looking for yourself, single believer, shall be a believer of Christ in obedience to the word of Paul in 2 Corinthians 6:14-15: *Be ye not unequally yoked together with unbelievers: for what fellowship hath righteousness with unrighteousness? and what communion hath light with darkness? And what concord hath Christ with Belial? or what part hath he that believeth with an infidel?* Failing to obey that commandment in having your spouse can mean destruction to your marriage and family. I heard many divorced ministers even in America feel sorry when they ignore this commandment in terms of choosing your spouse. Don't choose according to flesh; choose according to the will of God, and you will receive the promised blessings of God to be given to his people down to their family members, because they honor his word.

Renewing my covenant

Revelation 2:2-5: *I know thy works, and thy labour, and thy patience, and how thou canst not bear them which are evil: and thou hast tried them which say they are apostles, and are not, and hast found them liars: And hast borne, and hast patience, and for my name's sake hast laboured, and hast not fainted. Nevertheless I have somewhat against thee, because thou hast left thy first love. Remember therefore from whence thou art fallen, and repent, and do the first works; or else I will come unto thee quickly, and will remove thy candlestick out of his place, except thou repent.*

I loved my days in the Bible school. You know the feeling when you are in the right place at the right time doing the right things of GOD. I realized peace and comfort at those times from the Lord. The time that I decided to give up my networking business was also the time that my wife was pregnant with our first child, Gabriel. So, it wasn't that easy to lose that source of income, but the Lord strengthened me to trust only in Him. So, at the last semester that I had in the school, I surrendered that business and decided to trust God wholeheartedly by doing what he asked of me. Before this happened, God also reproved me. One day, I woke up with the back of my head aching. It was as if I was having a stroke. Of course, it probably wasn't, for I was very young to have a stroke. But who knows? I felt the pain, and was praying and asking God what was happening. Then I heard him tell me, "Who told you to go into this full-time (networking business) ministry? I'd never ask you to do that. Now, I want you to get out of it, and just follow me, or something worse will happen to you."

We read in John 5:14: *Afterward Jesus findeth him in the temple, and said unto him, Behold, thou art made whole: sin no more, lest a worse thing come unto thee.* God disciplined me so as to stop me from going out of his will ignorantly. This discipline might be hard and painful for a time, but nevertheless this is for our own good, because he loves us.

Our Bible school allowed me to study there even if I had no money, and decided to make me a student worker. They gave me an allowance for at least 250 a week (that amount can be just a meal for two in a fast food restaurant), and this made me to ask for more, and not being contented for a time, that made me to find money outside the Bible school. I forgot that I was there not to earn money, but to earn knowledge from him. In having this, I renewed my covenant with him, repented of the error that I did, and asked him to once again strengthen me, and this he did, and more than that, he again led me into all truth. Our failures today can be a learning to us and a message to the future if we will continue following Jesus.

Spiritual warfare

Ephesians 6:12-18: *For we wrestle not against flesh and blood, but against principalities, against powers, against the rulers of the darkness of this world, against spiritual wickedness in high places. Wherefore take unto you the whole armor of God, that ye may be able to withstand in the evil day, and having done all, to stand. Stand therefore, having your loins girt about with truth, and having on the breastplate of righteousness; And your feet shod with the preparation of the gospel of peace; Above all, taking the shield of faith, wherewith ye shall be able to quench all the fiery darts of the wicked.   And take the helmet of salvation, and the sword of the Spirit, which is the word of God: Praying always with all prayer and supplication in the Spirit, and watching thereunto with all perseverance and supplication for all saints.*

Spiritual warfare is the truth that often is denied and misunderstood by so many professing Christians. To some, it's not necessary, since according to them, Jesus already defeated Satan on a cross, and was resurrected, so we need only to rely on that "finished work of Jesus" and not fight again, for again they will say the "battle is the Lord's" and not ours. Those statements are half-truth and half error. Yes, Jesus already defeated sin on a cross, in order to do what man couldn't do so as pay the debt of sin (Romans 8:2-3). But it is wrong to say that we don't have to fight, since it's written in many passages of the Bible that we have to fight, and these are in the New Testament, even after Jesus finished his work on a cross. Allow me to verify this by at least two or three different passages. Remember that God told us that everything must be established by the mouth of two or three witnesses.

2 Corinthians 10:4-5: *(For the weapons of our warfare are not carnal, but mighty through God to the pulling down of strong holds;) Casting down imaginations, and every high thing that*

exalted itself against the knowledge of God, and bringing into captivity every thought to the obedience of Christ.

James 4:7: *Submit yourselves therefore to God. Resist the devil, and he will flee from you.*

1 Peter 5:8-9: *Be sober, be vigilant; because your adversary the devil, as a roaring lion, walketh about, seeking whom he may devour: Whom resist stedfast in the faith, knowing that the same afflictions are accomplished in your brethren that are in the world.*

The passages above are the evidence of the truth of the spiritual warfare that must be waged by us Christians, and failing to do this will result in a spiritual or physical damage of our life, family, and even ministry (people). God wants me to know of this truth, and even to give me knowledge and experiences of it. Knowledge must be put into an experience in order to become a wisdom. He provided me books and testimonies that were helpful for me to gain a deep understanding of this truth that Satan hides from the church. Spiritual ignorance will result in a destruction of the church, or even our lives, if it is not resolved. Satan's best weapon is deception. For you to be defeated by him, he will make you believe that he is not real, or not even powerful, or is not a threat to you, so as to make you complacent and negligent of your spiritual duty. This will result in spiritual damage. How many churches get destroyed by the enemy by not believing in spiritual warfare? How many husbands and wives get divorced because of the spirit of lust? How many pastors and church relationships were destroyed just because of the spirit of gossip and slander? How many pastors' associations are divided because of the spirit of envy, jealousy, and division? Peter, Paul and the other apostles were all aware of Satan's evil work. That's why they often guarded themselves and warned the churches during their lifetimes.

Spiritual books and testimonies

1 Thessalonians 5:21-22: *Prove all things; hold fast that which is good. Abstain from all appearance of evil.*

I read book after book (most were free) about spiritual warfare. Many were useful; some were not (for they were just theories and man-made ideas). I already mentioned the books of Mary K. Baxter (*A Divine Revelation of Heaven; A Divine Revelation of Hell*). I also read a book by Kenneth Hagin about understanding gifts and power. One book that I read was used by God to really awaken me. It was the testimony of Emmanuel Amos Eni entitled, *"Delivered from the Powers of Darkness"*. It's forty-five pages, and I read it in just three hours! His testimony was all about him being a powerful wizard, and how God saved him from that power. He explained in detail how they used to attack Christians in so many ways, and how they were able to get out of their physical bodies (astral projection) so as to go hovering in both the heavens and the earth, watching over people that were assigned to them by Satan, to be destroyed by them. He explained so many things that we need to know to gain an understanding of how spiritual warfare is being waged in the spiritual realm. He also testified of the saving power of Jesus and his blood on the believers. He said that we are known to be the true believers of Christ, not by means of our clothing, or the Bible that we carry, but the fire or the light of God in us! He also said how many carnal Christians were being used by Satan to distract others in the church. There are so many good things about this book, I recommend you to please read and study that testimony yourself.

Another book God used to educate me about spiritual warfare is the testimony of pastor Kim Yong Doo and his church's testimony. He wrote the series of books entitled, *"Baptized by Blazing Fire"*. I and some of our leaders read the series of this book (1-7), and studied them by the guidance of the Holy Spirit and by the knowledge we have from the Bible. Pastor Kim and his church were both blessed with their spiritual eyes and ears opened, enough for them to see heaven, hell, demons, angels, and mostly the trinity, God in the Spirit. That is an amazing revelation of the spiritual realm, and I learned a lot and even received some experiences that were similar to them when we began to flow in the Spirit. I also urge you to read them, and I thank God for giving us those books.

Of course, this book that I have written is not a shadow of those books, although it has a connection. God uses them to equip us, so as to give birth to another book that can be used by him to educate and empower his church until Jesus comes again.

Spiritual experiences

Galatians 1:11-12: *But I certify you, brethren, that the gospel which was preached of me is not after man. For I neither received it of man, neither was I taught it, but by the revelation of Jesus Christ.*

While I was in the last semester in the Bible school, and was reading the spiritual books, God allowed me to experience some spiritual encounters with the enemies in that place (for each and every place throughout the world has a demon or group of demons to guard it. Some call them territorial spirits). It happened while I was praying, and I saw this vision of a pair of eyes (it's demonic in form) that were staring at me, and then afterwards I fell asleep. Often when we are spiritually weak, the enemy can make us fall into dizziness and make us not able to get up our prayer into heaven (this is one of the reasons why some prayers have no answer; they are powerless). At that time, the students in the Bible school used to be in a quarrel with one another that almost led into a fist fight (some quarrels were only verbal fighting). The Lord told me that the pair of eyes that stared at me was the principality that guarded that school. It was also responsible for the quarrelling, and the sins being committed by the students in that place. It has the assignment from Satan to lure both the professors and the students into being carnal so as to not become a problem to them. That's why often pastors were afraid to send their members into the Bible school, upon knowing some students became prideful enough to argue with their pastors after having received a little knowledge from the school (for some pastors weren't able to study in the Bible school), and those students ended up going out of their church and following their favorite teacher that was being idolized by them. These evil things didn't just happen there, they happened everywhere. That's why you need to be careful whom you follow. It is good to follow a person if it is for the reason of following Jesus and not just the person himself. Yes, of course, there are different reasons why students began to get out of their churches even after studying in Bible school. Some were for good, but some were for evil. In my case, it was for good. It was for the sake of being able to follow Jesus closely in a way that I could do what he wanted me to do completely.

Another experience that I had in the Bible school was that, while I was praying (in tongues, with my hands lifted up), mice used to run to and fro overhead in the attic so as to create an annoying noise, for the purpose of distracting me. That was the first time that I heard them create such an annoying noise. In some instances, some student used to come to me in order to argue whether my prayer (speaking in tongues) was biblical or not, and this too was one of the attacks against me (Satan was just using this person, and that person might not have known it). One of the students testified that, in the middle of the night, he happened to wake up to walk to the restroom, then when he looked out the window, he saw an image of a black creature with wings on its side! After about half a minute, the creature was gone. He felt goose bumps and did not continue going on to the restroom. There also was a time that while I was reading a Bible, I smelled something that seemed like the smell of rotten flesh, and that time it was raining. It lasted about a minute, and then suddenly it was gone. Some students also managed to smell it and wondered what it was.

Experience after experience are provided by the Lord so as to equip us, and we only have to be aware of them. Everything happens for a reason; we all know that.

Getting out of them, going on to Jesus

Luke 5:8-1: *When Simon Peter saw it, he fell down at Jesus' knees, saying, Depart from me; for I am a sinful man, O Lord. For he was astonished, and all that were with him, at the draught of the fishes which they had taken: And so was also James, and John, the sons of Zebedee, which were partners with Simon. And Jesus said unto Simon, Fear not; from henceforth thou shalt catch men. And when they had brought their ships to land, they forsook all, and followed him.*

The call of Jesus to leave everything behind is a must and should be our priority. But often many hesitate in following his call for so many reasons, and this makes them become unfruitful - notable to provide the fruit that God requires. However, to those that will and are now following him, they will receive an eternal inheritance in heaven, and the glory that never fades shall be theirs forever and ever.

After I graduated from the Bible school, I still wanted to return to my former church, for I had the thought of wanting to help them with the knowledge that I have. When my pastor asked me of my motive of going into the Bible school, I told him that I wanted to be learning more, so that I may be able to help the church more. This reason seemed not that important to him, so much so that we ended up parting our ways. Maybe to him I wasn't that important; nevertheless, I believe that this was God's way of leading me to go and follow him by leaving everything behind. Remember that in the scripture above, the disciples "left all (the net, the boat, the fish, and their father)" so as to follow Jesus. So, I got out of my former church so as to get into the place where Jesus is, and it wasn't that easy at first. Nothing is easy when we truly decide to follow Jesus; it will be costly. My friends didn't agree with me, and some of my classmates even tried to change my decision. But I told them, it's not my own decision, or the church's, but the Lord's, so that they silenced themselves.

Follow Jesus, not men

1 Corinthians 7:23: *Ye are bought with a price; be not ye the servants of men.*

After my graduation from the Bible school, the thought came of asking, "Now what, or, where, Lord, do you want us to begin our ministry?" It used to fill my mind. We believe that God knows our future, so we are to determine to ask him of our future and how we may be able to get there. Out of 603,550 soldiers that were numbered by Moses, those that were twenty years old and up that could fight on the battle field (Numbers 1:45-46), only two of them managed to get into the land of Canaan so as to possess their inheritance. These two (and their families) were Joshua and Caleb; the rest died due to unbelief (Hebrews 3:19). All of them rejected God's word, and we don't want to commit the same mistake so as to experience the same failure. We have to determine to really follow Jesus and not men.

My wife and I at this point in time (after I graduated from the Bible school) were both praying and looking for a ministry, a church to begin our spiritual work with the Lord together. Three ministries/churches were being offered to us; first, one of the Baptist churches at Taysan Batangas. They offered a minimum of ten thousand pesos monthly allowance, with a free pastoral house (water and electric bill included). As I was pondering the benefits, I almost believed that this was the will of God for us to begin our ministry. That church had called me to be their youth pastor as I was studying in the Bible school. They were planning to remove the former pastor due to their unsatisfactory evaluation of his service. Some churches run their ministry having a secular point of view. They hire and fire pastors, some for evil reasons, and some for good. However, this is not God's will. No pastor is perfect; therefore, they need grace from both God and the church to help them up in times of their falling. As I decided to accept the offer (the chairman of the board used to offer me their church even before I graduated from the Bible school, and even promised me things, for he is a business man), God immediately whispered into my ears and said, "Will you just be there for the sake of material benefits?" Then, in hearing that, I understood that God disapproved of my going to that church. So again, we waited and prayed for God's perfect ministry, place, and people. The second ministry that was offered to us was coming from a Nigerian missionary that is based on San Pablo City (Laguna). Our administrator introduced me to him, and then we talked about ministry, and he said that he wanted me to first attend their fellowships for a couple of times, for me to be able to see whether I would fit in to work with them. My wife and I attended their Sunday worship for three consecutive Sundays. The worship (singing) is good, and the preaching seemed like it was powerful (they are a Pentecostal church). So, I thought, this could be a good church for us, although I had a feeling that there was something that was missing. While I was praying to God about this something that was missing by them, immediately God gave me the passage of 1 Corinthians 13:1-3: *Though I speak with the tongues of men and of angels, and have not charity, I am become as sounding brass, or a tinkling cymbal. And though I have the gift of prophecy, and understand all mysteries, and all knowledge; and though I have all faith, so that I could remove mountains, and have not charity, I am nothing. And though I bestow all my goods to feed the poor, and though I give my body to be burned, and have not charity, it profiteth me nothing.*

So, the singing was good, the preaching was powerful, but they missed love. Or should I say that they have no love in what they are doing, and the Lord provided me the evidence of this truth by way of observation/discernment. Discerning people just listen to God in order to know all things that they need to know, even without asking people. (Discernment is our God-given spiritual ability to know people, and often hidden things that we need to know by way of special revelation in order to help them come into the knowledge of God). Jesus had this discernment (John 2:24-25). I discerned that this Nigerian pastor had no love for his co-workers; he was treating them as if they were his slaves! So, when he told to us to begin our ministry with them, with him to be our leader, God on our way home again whispered into my ear and said, "If you will work with him, you will not be able to do the things that I will entrust to you." When we got home, I shared this message from the Lord with my wife. I was surprised that she had also received the same message that I received from the Lord. This made us to once again reject them, since God rejected them. We servants of God should learn to reject what the Lord has already rejected, and to accept what he has accepted. Often, many of us do the contrary, to our hurt. Gehazi, Elisha's assistant, received what the Lord had rejected, the gift which was the pride of Naaman (2 Kings 5:20-27), thereby receiving the leprosy of Naaman. This also was passed on to his descendants forever (verse 27). On the other hand, Peter rejected what the Lord had accepted. In one of his visions (Acts 10:9-48) while he was praying, God commanded him to rise up, kill and eat the forbidden animals (according to their tradition), but he rejected God's command for the sake of his tradition. But God rebuked him by saying, "Don't consider unclean things that have been made clean by God", and this made him to realize that God wanted him to go to the house of a gentile, Cornelius, which also was a believer, in order to preach the gospel unto them, and baptize them. We have to be very careful to consider God's will to obey, and not just our own mind.

The second ministry that was offered to us was rejected by us, even after the Nigerian pastor got disappointed in us, and we again waited, praying for God's will to be done in regard to our ministry.

The third offer of ministry came from the group of pastors that were former students of the Bible school. They asked me to join their group, even by the persuasion of our administrator, for he was a spiritual leader of this group. When I decided to accept their offer, and even thought that this maybe the right group to begin our ministry, yet the Lord in his mercy once again told us to not participate with them, and he gave me the scripture above (1 Corinthians 7:23). This was the third time, and still God didn't approve any of them. I remember when prophet Samuel was being commanded by God to go into the house of Jesse in order to anoint the person that would take over the authority of being king that was being removed from Saul (1 Samuel16:1-13). Samuel at first chose Eliab. Upon seeing his stature, he thought that he was the right one (verses 6-7), but God gently corrected him by saying, *Look not on his countenance, or on the height of his stature; because I have refused him: for the LORD seeth not as man seeth; for man looketh on the outward appearance, but the LORD looketh on the heart.* Samuel had to wait patiently eight times, until he had met the right one, David, a man after God's own heart (verses 12-13). Likewise, we also must learn of this lesson of waiting for the right man, ministry, and timing for God's will to be done. We did it, and the Lord directed us specifically to have a ministry that is approved by him. Now we have this ministry: "Christ the Living Word Fire Ministry". I praise God for setting our feet in the right direction for this ministry. For many are zealous in their work, in the ministry of the Lord, but very few have knowledge.

The kingdom of power

1 Corinthians 4:20*: For the kingdom of God is not in word, but in power.*

Acts 1:8: *But ye shall receive power, after that the Holy Ghost is come upon you: and ye shall be witnesses unto me both in Jerusalem, and in all Judaea, and in Samaria, and unto the uttermost part of the earth.*

The power of the kingdom of God is what has been promised by God to all of his followers. Jesus promised this to his disciples as stated above, Elisha asked this of Elijah, Moses had this so as to deliver Israel from Pharaoh, judges ruled and protected God's people through this power, and this is supposed to be sought for by his people nowadays.

The Lord began his earthly ministry being filled by the power of the Holy Spirit. By that power he cast out demons, performed miracles, and preached and taught the kingdom of God to people in a way that their futile human minds, even their filled-up traditional knowledge couldn't fathom, nor deny. People clearly saw the difference between the work of Jesus and the work of the Pharisees. Matthew 9:8: *But when the multitudes saw it, they marvelled, and glorified God, which had given such power unto men.*

Three ministries were offered to us. Some came into our mind, so we thought that those were the right one to work with. God, however, in his divine wisdom and mercy, rejected them all because he had in mind a much greater ministry (for us), a kind of ministry that is built on him as its foundation, and the power of the Spirit to recognize its authority. Often, we people tend to be impatient and try to get on ahead of God, yet praise God, he often gently guides us not to be misled by our own understanding, for there is always a consequence for every failure. God will never be shaken by the things that shake us. He knows everything; truth that we know (about him) is rarely understood by us. We tend to listen to our minds, our physical circumstances, and people around us, and thereby we base decisions on our own judgment, and often we get hurt by that wrong judgment, and that wrong judgment comes from our own failure to listen to only him. How many lives have been wasted because of the failure to listen to God's instructions?   Untimely death is the great penalty for this kind of stubbornness.

After I graduated from the Bible school, and the Lord rejected the ministries offered to us, we still waited patiently upon the Lord. We decided to hope only in the Lord, although some of our friends used to worry for us, but the Lord never did.

The first test ministry

Luke 16:10: *He that is faithful in that which is least is faithful also in much: and he that is unjust in the least is unjust also in much.*

Faithfulness is God's measurement of our work with him, whether it will last, or be just for a while. Our motive, reasoning, and character are all known to him.

God led me to take a first step of beginning our ministry at one place in Famy Laguna. It was being offered to me by one of my classmates in the Bible school, who is older than I am. I received the offer, and began to serve God in that place for almost two years. Since my family was far from that place, I alone used to be there from Friday noon to Monday morning. While I was there, during that time, my mother already went home here in the Philippines, and within a month of her stay here God moved her heart, and she became a believer. Because of that we used to gather in our house every Monday night up to Thursday night in a prayer meeting. During those times, we all were reading the series of books by Pastor Kim Yong Doo entitled *"Baptized by Blazing Fire"*, and in my extra time I also was reading the books by prophet Rick Joyner entitled: *"The Call"* and *"The Final Quest"*. It seemed that each book has its own theme and emphases; I praise God for giving them to me. In just a short time after our mother's conversion, God wrought extraordinary experiences with her, and with all of those that attended our every night prayer meetings. Visions of hell, heaven, angels, demons, the future, and God himself were being shown by God to us from time to time.

In the ministry at Famy Laguna, we also received God's power in that place as we earnestly pled to God to clothe us with the power from above. Both the adults and the children received this power of God, and God also provided them extraordinary spiritual experiences, such as visions, dreams, prophecy, deliverance, and open spiritual eyes (the ability to see the current spiritual realm with your spiritual eyes).

The beginning of power: fire baptism

Matthew 3:11: *I indeed baptize you with water unto repentance: but he that cometh after me is mightier than I, whose shoes I am not worthy to bear: he shall baptize you with the Holy Ghost, and with fire.*

Acts 2:2-4: *And suddenly there came a sound from heaven as of a rushing mighty wind, and it filled all the house where they were sitting. And there appeared unto them cloven tongues like as of fire, and it sat upon each of them. And they were all filled with the Holy Ghost, and began to speak with other tongues, as the Spirit gave them utterance.*

The holy fire of God is the power that, according to Jesus, is greatly feared by the devil. Snakes really don't like fire. This power helps us realize the truth of our spiritual life. Jesus helps us to be cleansed by it, and through it he awakens and strengthens our spiritual senses, things that Satan doesn't want to happen to Christians. How many Christians nowadays live being defeated by Satan because of not having the power of God - some due to ignorance, while some due to unbelief. Satan would love to give you much physical work if that is what would make you spiritually weak. He even is willing to give you money and fame if that will make you focus on your flesh and not on the power of the Spirit. Many people argue and boast of their fleshly work, achievements, and traditions to each other. This often leads to confusion and division. God requires people to live by the leading of the Spirit, and not to rely on the flesh. Just when I began to follow God I used to hear and see God's power in others, and in hearing about them, God led me to seek for it myself. That made me to really be willing to give up everything just to receive what God promises me in his word. As I read the Bible, I saw great men of God walking in power, and this made me get excited to experience this myself.

God has an appointed time for everything under the sun, and he makes it beautiful in his own time (Ecclesiastes 3:1,11). It's also the same in terms of giving this power. God is not in a hurry to give his power (and gifts) to his people, for once it will be given it can't be taken back.

As I read the books of Fire Baptism, I was blessed; praise God! Blessed with knowledge, revelations, and also experience. While I was reading them, I had my Bible beside me to make sure of their truthfulness, for many books are misleading. One way of God confirming things to us is through direct inquiry. It's like me asking God about something, and he will give his answer to the prophets (my mother is one of them). In the Old Testament and even in the New Testament this also was the way of the church's direct dealing with the Lord. Although now, many don't approve of this kind of direct communication with God through inquiry, but we did this. There is no such word in the Bible that he gave to his people to stop this kind of direct communication with him; on the contrary, he encourages them to do so. We read in many passages, *"He that hath an ear, let him hear what the Spirit saith unto the churches"*.

My personal experience of fire baptism

1 Peter1:3-5: *Blessed be the God and Father of our Lord Jesus Christ, which according to his abundant mercy hath begotten us again unto a lively hope by the resurrection of Jesus Christ from the dead, To an inheritance incorruptible, and undefiled, and that fadeth not away, reserved in heaven for you, Who are kept by the power of God through faith unto salvation ready to be revealed in the last time.*

As I began reading the books of Fire Baptism, I also was expectant and prayerful so as to receive it myself. One night while I was praying with my hands lifted up to heaven, I was asking God to bless me with this power, and without fail he gave it to me. I felt something flow down on my body from the tips of my fingers down to my hands, arms, head, and whole body. I shook uncontrollably! The experience was real, as real as when I touch something physically. My prayer that night took two hours! Before I used to pray for just ten to fifteen minutes within my mind, but after I was baptized by fire, it was lengthened from one hour to three hours! Yes, now because of deception in teaching, and the worries of this life, believers usually fail praying for even an hour daily! No wonder that very rarely they receive a breakthrough in their spiritual lives.

My experience went on. While praying to God for a long hour in tongues, I continually got filled by God's power. In my prayer, there were times that my body was sweating, and my shirt was drenched by the water from my body that went out, since I felt hot within my body. It's as if you were praying in the middle of the day, and your body was sweating because of the heat, yet it was nighttime, and I had a fan before me. While praying, I was listening to myself, although I was ignorant of the languages, and by that I was able to observe the reactions of my body. My voice sometimes went deeper and big. Sometimes I observed that I was singing in my praying in tongues, sometimes it was warfare, and sometimes it was an intercession. Your spirit will know all things because of the Holy Spirit that testifies inside. We know that prayer has different forms. Even after praying for a long hour, I got energized even physically. You will be exhausted for a while after your prayer, but you can immediately get back your physical strength as if nothing had happened. Some of our members that used to attend our prayer meeting were working at SM Mall. They used to be with us, beginning at 11:00 p.m. And we finished at 1:00 a.m., and they got home at 3:00 a.m., and they had to go to their work at 10:00 a.m., and according to them they never got sleepy or felt tired in the store, even after praying with us at night. This took place for months, until God gave us another direction.

The more we become spiritually sensitive, the more we will become the primary target of our enemy, the devil. Satan knows what is happening all around the world, as their god, and in the churches, as their accuser. Demons go to and from hell to the earth so as to report to him the events that are taking place. I found out that Satan's demonic works are much more focused on the churches, for if he will succeed in destroying them, there is no one to stop him in all of his evil agendas.

The evil work of Satan

1 Timothy 5:15: *For some are already turned aside after Satan.*

Satan has many evil strategies so as to pull us down. One of these strategies is to make the church leaders be divided, to the point of removing their pastor. There are many reasons why churches remove their pastors, but as for me it is not the will of God for the church to do that to their pastor, though we all know that pastors can commit mistakes, since they are still human. Yet, the church must learn to forgive and restore their pastor as they help him to stand up again after his falling down, and failing to do this can be a huge sin against the Lord that has sent this man as his messenger.

In Famy, the church members, even the children, including the teenagers, were all blessed by God with the power of fire, and likewise had their spiritual eyes and ears opened by God. Some leaders also were blessed with the gift of prophecy. But we have to understand that the more we receive spiritual blessings from God, the more that Satan will target us - that is if he can't hinder you from receiving the power, he will at least try to corrupt you so as to twist the power. If that happens, it's like him using you to aim your weapon against your comrade, and this is a disastrous sight. This happened to us in Famy. One of the leaders, a woman, was blessed by the gift of prophecy, visions, and hand signs movement. In having those power and gifts, I often told the church to be prayerful, and always read the Bible, and to be pure in their hearts and minds since the enemy is always watching us like a roaring lion seeking an opportunity to devour us (1 Peter 5:8). It happened that this woman held a grudge in her heart toward her husband (her husband is also one of our leaders), and she failed to continually forgive him, and this served as an open door for Satan to occupy her. First, it was through her emotions, then, little by little, inside her heart. In having this demonic oppression from

Satan, she still was too stubborn to consider my advice to her as her pastor, and it happened that she began to attack me by giving a false message that, according to her, was from God, yet when I observed it, and by the help of God, I saw that it was just her own presumption. It was weeks and months that she stayed in that deception, and she even did things out of order. Her husband, one of my leaders, told me to confront her to stop these wrong actions, for it was creating confusion in the people. One of those wrong things was that, in the middle of the preaching of the word, she would stand up and take one member in a corner of the church, for according to her, she received a word from God. Then suddenly, she would begin to speak in tongues, move her hands in different directions, perform deliverance - all while I was preaching. This made some of our people get distracted by her. Another one of these false workings occurred while we were praying, all of us together with the youth, standing and praying in tongues with our eyes closed. I was in front declaring God's word in prayer, and then suddenly she went in front before me and performed her own prayer of warfare against me. I know this because she was aiming her hands toward me. This was seen by her husband, who was there at that time. She did this while her eyes were closed, so I was looking at her, and then I walked toward the corner little by little (without her noticing it, for her eyes were closed), then when she opened her eyes and saw nothing there, she stopped what she was doing and returned to her place. Prior to that, as we begin our prayer meeting that night, she stood on her seat shouting at us saying, "(calling her husband's name) repent! You Joven, repent!" This was quite obviously of the work of Satan, although the person might not be that fully aware of it. This deception went on until she called for a leaders' meeting on her own, because according to her, God gave her a message, and she wrote it all down on one page of yellow paper. We attended (we were four) and even read the message. Her husband took from her the message and read it, then gave it to us to read, and to our surprise, all of the content of that message were the things that according to her, were my fault! It seemed that she recorded all of my wrongs (things that were wrong just according to her own mind). We know that according to 1 Corinthians 13:5, love keeps no record of wrong, so this was quite clear that the spirit that was giving the message to this woman was not from God, and she failed to test it. She even said that God told her to remove the authority of a pastor from me, and she said that God was going to transfer it to someone that would be chosen by her within the group, and we (the three of us) concluded that she would say it would be hers to receive. Her husband confronted her gently, trying to persuade her of the error that was happening to her due to her failure of testing the spirit. She walked out of that meeting yelling at us, she even angrily pointed her finger before my face and threw a curse on me. By that time, I was just peaceful by the grace of God. We three left that meeting discussing how we would be able to fix this problem. Two of them were confused on what to do. They were not that fully convinced of the deception that was taking place, in spite of the manner that was being displayed by her (remember that a tree can be known by its own fruit). We prayed that night for God's confirmation, whether he was the one that gave the message of removing me from authority, or if it was the enemy. Then, God gave a vision to one of the leaders, telling us of the deception that happened. Sadly, even after this confirmation, they were still undecided as to whether to ignore the deception or to listen to it. The next day, as I was about to go home, I was praying to God for his instructions regarding the things that I supposed to do. God gave me a word from the Bible that told me, rise up, pick up your things, and go home! This meant that I had to leave them, and this saddened my heart, for I was thinking about the young ones of that church. The message was confirmed when the husband of that woman called me and said that they had decided to remove me from being a pastor. I prayed for forgiveness for them, and blessed them, and entrusted them to the Lord. But this experience really hurt me, for I love them, and had a dream of a glorious future with them.

After this destructive work of Satan against us, by succeeding in dividing us, God declared to us that he would be protecting the young ones from the spirit of deception that the leaders accepted. After this, my family and I, and the friends that used to attend our every night prayer meeting, gathered and decided to ask God for instructions. For a time, we happened to attend a Sunday fellowship at a nearby church while waiting for the Lord. The church that we attended was one of the branches of the well-known church here in the Philippines. This church, like my former church (when I was a youth) had implemented a man-made system that has a goal of multiplying the number of their members year by year - even trying to put pressure on their workers so as to meet the target number. This sounds like Pharaoh at the time of Moses.

The Lord directed our path

Psalms 32:*8: I will instruct thee and teach thee in the way which thou shalt go: I will guide thee with mine eye.*

As he promises, the Lord performs it; he guides us in every step that we make as we continually follow his word. In our pursuit of the ministry the Lord would give to us, and the place to do it, he led us supernaturally. Since the Lord blesses the church with the prophetic gifts and power, through those gifts and power we are able to communicate with the Lord directly. We can do an inquiry; it's a direct contact with him by means of one of our prophetesses (often it was Prophetisa) so as to confirm a thing or a plan, whether it was his will or not, for we are not foolish so as to go alone to a place doing a thing without the Lord's presence to abide in us. This was one of Moses' wise requests to the Lord when he was talking to him on Mount Sinai (Exodus 33:13-17).   The Lord led us to move from one place to another so as to be trained by means of having a different experience in each and every place. On September 6, 2013, we left Los Banos Laguna (we sold our little house there) to transfer to barangay Sucol Calamba Laguna. The house in which we lived there was an old and abandoned house. We perceived that it was the oldest house there. We rented that house, in spite of it being said that it was a place for ghosts; some called it a haunted house. We found that place miraculously. I believe the Lord wants me to put in detail how we ended up going into that old house.

Directed through dreams, prophecy, and visions

From Los Banos to Calamba, from Calamba to Bay, from Bay to Los Banos again…

Genesis 12:1 – 4: *Now the LORD had said unto Abram, Get thee out of thy country, and from thy kindred, and from thy father's house, unto a land that I will shew thee: And I will make of thee a great nation, and I will bless thee, and make thy name great; and thou shalt be a blessing: And I will bless them that bless thee, and curse him that curseth thee: and in thee shall all families of the earth be blessed. So Abram departed, as the LORD had spoken unto him; and Lot went with him: and Abram was seventy and five years old when he departed out of Haran.*

After our every night prayer meeting at Los Banos, the Lord directed us to go and leave this place and transfer to another. He didn't give us the name of the place which we were to go to (at first). He just gave us a picture of some portion of the house and its color and design, in a dream and a vision of our members. Every picture in a dream and vision can be likened to a piece of a puzzle that we gathered so as to make the whole picture. At God's leading, we searched the entire city of Los Banos in search of that house (there are almost 20,000 different houses in this town!). We even went to a place that we hadn't been for years in our stay in this city. For a week, we almost searched the fourteen barangays of this city, only to find nothing. Then one day we were praying, and then the three of us decided to go again so as to search for this house, this time to the next city, Calamba. Just before we went out of the house, the Lord instructed my wife, April Joy, that we should stay, and have our rest, for the Lord would be the one to provide what we were looking for. Sadly, we ignored it. We went walking from barangay Timugan up to the next city, Calamba. When we reached its first barangay, Masili, we decided to rest, then suddenly I received a call. It was from my classmate in Bible school (Senen San Antonio) and he lived in barangay Sucol, next to barangay Masili. He called me and said that he was in our rented house at Los Banos, and he just wanted to visit me. We three (I, April Joy, and sister Rizalie) decided to go back home, and found Senen waiting for us. We talked for a while and found out that his visit was just a casual one, nothing important. I told him that we were at the barangay Masili next to them when he called me, and told him that we were looking for an old house to rent since we were planning to transfer there. He told us that his uncle's house was an old house and it was just close to them. He even gave us the details of the house, and to our surprise, his descriptions fit the picture of the old house that God gave to us in dreams and visions! We read how Peter was led by God to find the meaning of his vision by God sending him the three men of Cornelius. Our eyes were shining brightly as if we saw already what we were looking for. We decided to schedule the day to visit the house, and Senen went home. When we three pondered of these things my wife said, "This is what the Lord meant when said to us to rest, for he will provide what we were looking for!" Though we were a bit dismayed that we ignored his message, and wasted our strength, we still were thankful that he fulfills his word! Praise God.

The day when we visited the house, our conviction was very strong that this really was the one that we were looking for. The house was old, the windows were broken (an old type wooden window with sea shells as its decoration), the dividing walls made of wood were all destroyed, and holes from the roof allowed the rainwater to get inside, and that made both the floor and the ceiling to be broken. The surrounding area was filled with garbage, since the last people to stay in this house used it as a junk shop. I talked to the sister of the real owner, and we agreed to rent the house (although its price didn't fit its condition).

We transferred to that house on September 6, 2013, and we went out from there on September 5, 2015. All of those that went out from Los Banos to follow us there were challenged to go on in a full-time ministry. Excitement and joy filled our hearts and minds so that we were not thinking of the things that we would experience in that place. All of us, together with my family, and the other workers of the church, lived in that old house together. We all had only one thing in mind - to serve the Lord whole-heartedly.

As I was reading how the Israelites were led by God through Moses, with signs and wonders, a pillar of fire at night and a cloud by day, I saw God there walking with them intimately, and this intimate relationship with the Lord is what we are seeking for. God led us to move from Los Banos to Calamba, and after our time was finished there, we were being led to even transfer to Bay Laguna. You may ask, why? Our answer is that, only God knows. Yet our stay in those places was filled with powerful experiences, and trust and struggling day by day, that we only were able to overcome by his grace.

Spiritual gifts and power developed and increased daily

Acts 2:42-47: *And they continued stedfastly in the apostles' doctrine and fellowship, and in breaking of bread, and in prayers. And fear came upon every soul: and many wonders and signs were done by the apostles. And all that believed were together, and had all things common; And sold their possessions and goods, and parted them to all men, as every man had need. And they, continuing daily with one accord in the temple, and breaking bread from house to house, did eat their meat with gladness and singleness of heart, Praising God, and having favour with all the people. And the Lord added to the church daily such as should be saved.*

While at Calamba, day by day we used to pray, and study the Bible in that place. We thought of nothing but to know the Lord more. As I was looking at the passionate will of the people to serve God, I was challenged, and was encouraged more. The Lord blessed us with the prophetic gifts and power in that place and even strengthened what was already in us. Our spiritual ability was utilized, and our minds were renewed daily. As the Lord provided us the spiritual power and experiences, our hearts and minds were both focused on those spiritual things, and were little by little being removed from the things of the world. That house was like a spiritual training place for us! I remember one of the sisters that visited us, say she was seeking for the Lord, and she asked me why the Lord brought us to that place (during that time we had no electricity). My answer was: "I thank God that he brought us here!" The spiritual training that we had there can't easily be found anywhere else outside; even in the place that most believers went in to have a fellowship. The house/place was like a hidden treasure from the eyes of an ordinary human; even believers, yet it was known to those whom the Lord chose to see it as he sees it! When the twelve spies were sent by Moses to Canaan, ten of them saw the giants of problems that they would be facing; yet only Joshua and Caleb saw the giant blessings that were in that place, by the eyes of faith! Truly, God's blessings often are hidden from the natural person, yet are fully opened to the spiritual one (1 Corinthians 2:6-16). As days went by, the Lord opened both the spiritual eyes and ears of our members (we were almost twenty adults there, with ten children), and they began to see and even hear things that couldn't be seen by the natural eyes. Spiritual things can only be perceived spiritually. Every time we prayed our members saw and experienced the spiritual world. They began to see angels assisting us in prayers. Some of them had just a pair of wings, some had two pairs, and others had three pairs. The Lord declared to us that since the pastor and the leaders were in charge, with much more heavy spiritual tasks, that Satan was sending more powerful demons against them than the ones he sent to the little ones in the church, so God assigned to them seraphim (angels who have two and three pairs of wings). As Satan assigns an evil spirit to blind an unbeliever, God on the other hand assigns an angel to guard a believer until the day that person would get out of this world. Not just angels are present every time we are praying or worshipping the Lord in any time at any form; demons are also present to distract us in any possible way (1 Samuel 7:7-12). These things were being shown to us by the Lord. As the Lord opened their spiritual senses, they also at the same became prone as targets to the enemy. Satan will do everything so as to close what the Lord has opened in our lives, yet as we obey God, he will end up defeated (Revelation 3:7-8). God mobilizes us in a variety of ways. Some he trains to become ears so as to open their spiritual ears (audibly, and through the mind/heart; we call it the still small voice), and others are trained to be eyes, allowing them to see the spiritual world, and others are the feet so as to walk out the work of the Lord, and others are the hands so as to do the things of God, and some, like me, are the mouthpiece of God so as to speak the message of God. The adults, the youth, and the children all had their own unique experiences of having their eyes and ears and smelling be opened up to the spiritual realm. At one of our prayer meetings, while we were worshipping the Lord, all of us smelled a sweet fragrance that we found out to be the scent of heaven. The smell was as real as the fragrance the women use, yet it's not from us; it's from the Lord. We were all happy, exclaiming praises to God as he allowed us to experience such a supernatural event. This experience helped us understand the reality of heaven. One would not easily believe by words, so the Lord in his mercy provides us an actual experience, and this not just once, but many happened to us that are difficult to explain, and these things are true and not just an illusion or a heresy.

The reason why God gave each and every one a unique experience and spiritual abilities, is so that none should get into a competition that would result in division, and that each should learn to complement each other. Sadly, due to lack of knowledge, Satan deluded many, and provoked them to fight one another.

Being insulted and maligned because of Jesus

Matthew 5:11-12: *Blessed are ye, when men shall revile you, and persecute you, and shall say all manner of evil against you falsely, for my sake. Rejoice, and be exceeding glad: for great is your reward in heaven: for so persecuted they the prophets which were before you.*

The sister that used to talk to us on behalf of the owner of the house, who was her brother, tended to treat us harshly due to our delayed payment of the rental fee. Every time she came to speak to me, and asked for the rental fee, and received none, she ended up getting angry with me, and even used foul-mouthed words against me, and yelled so that people around us were looking at us.

I was humiliated by her, although I know that she just didn't know what she was doing. For months, things happened that way, and there were times I tried to hide myself when I knew that she was there and was looking for me to again ask me for the money. Sometimes I asked my mother to face her since I couldn't endure her angry presence, and she did not believe my words. I told her that we were just still looking for the way to find the money to pay them (since during that time, only my wife and some of our people were working, since the rest of us were in the full-time ministry, and this was hardly accepted by the other believers from other churches, since it was too difficult for them to obey the Lord in this way). The last month that I stayed with them, my wife managed to gather money (although it was just a tenth of the whole sum of our rental fee) and we gave it to them, promising to pay them the rest when the Lord would bless us. That sister even made me write a promissory note, with my name and signature in it. Sometimes, Christians are not true to their faith when there is money involved. This professing sister wasn't able to see how we managed to take care of their old house for two years, and that if we hadn't, it possibly could be destroyed by super typhoons. Yet, who cares? And we again continued our journey with the Lord.

Our next place: Bay Laguna

Exodus 19:1-5: *In the third month, when the children of Israel were gone forth out of the land of Egypt, the same day came they into the wilderness of Sinai. For they were departed from Rephidim, and were come to the desert of Sinai, and had pitched in the wilderness; and there Israel camped before the mount. And Moses went up unto God, and the LORD called unto him out of the mountain, saying, Thus shalt thou say to the house of Jacob, and tell the children of Israel; Ye have seen what I did unto the Egyptians, and how I bare you on eagles' wings, and brought you unto myself. Now therefore, if ye will obey my voice indeed, and keep my covenant, then ye shall be a peculiar treasure unto me above all people: for all the earth is mine.*

After our training time was finished at Calamba, we were directed by God to again transfer to Bay Laguna, a city next to Los Banos. In looking again for a house to rent, the Lord showed us some signs and colors that we were to search for so as to determine the right place to dwell in. We were determined to look for and find this house, and didn't want to be misled; failing to find the next target place is also a failure to receive the spiritual blessings that God has prepared for that place.

God just showed us a vision of an old house that had a rice field at the back of it, with pink ribbon tied on its door (I remember Rahab tied a rope on her window as a sign to the Israelites). We decided to search through the city of Bay, and after so many days, God led us the right way, and to the right people to speak to. We found the place and the man that directed us to the house, yet the first time that I observed the house, trying to compare it to the visions that were given to us, I concluded, this was not the right one. Miraculously, God made me to see the pink ribbon tied on its door. When the other searching team looked for the house that we were to dwell in (I was not with them), God directed them to the house that we already saw, a house that had a pink ribbon tied on its door, and they were all convicted that this was the right one. I was amazed and a little confused because, I had already seen that one, yet it didn't fit the description of the house when I compared it to the visions that were shown to us. This made me to inquire of the Lord, and his response was, "The vision that I gave you was the old structure of that house, and I didn't say that you are to still look for the same old picture of it; yet I gave you one of the signs that would make you not be misled; the pink ribbon tied on its door!" I praise God for his divine providence of guiding us to this next place that he commanded us to go.

At Bay Laguna

Joshua 5:1: *And it came to pass, when all the kings of the Amorites, which were on the side of Jordan westward, and all the kings of the Canaanites, which were by the sea, heard that the LORD had dried up the waters of Jordan from before the children of Israel, until we were passed over, that their heart melted, neither was there spirit in them anymore, because of the children of Israel.*

In spite of the circumstances (lack of money, comrades that left us, doubt in the minds of others) we, by the grace of God, managed to cross from Calamba to Bay Laguna. In comparison to the people of barangay Sucol of Calamba, the inhabitants of barangay San Antonio Bay were peaceful; they seemed like they were more focused on their own lives, rather than the gossipy and troubled people of barangay Sucol, Calamba Laguna, yet the Lord instructed to us to be discerning. Silent enemies are more dangerous than the noisy ones. The Lord also revealed to us that there were Satanists in that place, and they were fully aware of our coming. We even saw and heard a group of them praying a demonic ritual in the middle of the day, wearing black clothing! There were a few changes in the place that we were in compared to our former training place.   At Sucol Calamba, we had no electricity, gadgets, or appliances for almost two years, yet at Bay, we had them one by one. The Lord little by little provided us the things that we lost when we came to Sucol Calamba: TV, electric fan, cell phones, etc. When there is a change in the physical, there surely is a change also in the spiritual; the question is, is it a good change?

Since we again got involved with the things of the world, our passionate prayers, and studying of the word began to weaken little by little. Our time in the spirit was being stolen unknowingly by our time spent in the physical, having the things of the world. The fire of God inside us that was being fanned aflame by the passionate hours of prayer and studying of the word began to little by little die out! This called for an emergency spiritual alarm! The young people began to get involved again in the things that they once denied: social media! The older women began to watch TV, and these things were harming their spirituality. This made me to worry, and call upon the Lord for help. The Lord replied to me, and said, "Just before these things would come, I already knew it. Yet I allowed it for all of you to learn how to seek me in the dark, and how to seek me in the light. You learned to follow me out of nothingness (of material), now I will begin to train you to follow me out of abundance (of material things)! Upon hearing this, I determined to still lead the church people (that became half in number, the other half already went back into the world) to pray every night, and to encourage them to study the word of God.

Spiritual encounters

Acts 14:19-20: *And there came thither certain Jews from Antioch and Iconium, who persuaded the people, and, having stoned Paul, drew him out of the city, supposing he had been dead. Howbeit, as the disciples stood round about him, he rose up, and came into the city: and the next day he departed with Barnabas to Derbe.*

When we transferred to our next target place, the demons that used to battle us at Calamba pursued us at Bay, even to carry with them their human slaves that often were in a form of a spirit. These human spirits used to come to us trying to destroy us in any way possible as they did before. One night when I happened to wake up from my sleep, it was about 1a.m., and I was sitting at the front of our room, facing the room of our grandmother, where the children were also. I happened to see an image of a man standing before me, and knew that he was looking at me. He was in a form of a shadow, and I couldn't see his face since all the lights were off. At first, I thought he was our eldest brother (Rufino), but when I observed his height, he was taller than him, so I found out it wasn't him. So, for almost five minutes, we were looking at each other, although it was dark, and everyone was already sleeping. When I tried to stand up, he ran swiftly inside the room without making any noise! I tried to follow him, and even tried to turn on the light in that room, only to find all in that room deeply sleeping. I found out that this man was a visitor that Satan used to test us that night. This man in a form of a shadow was gone before me in a blink of an eye! I later found out that human spirits can move swiftly everywhere, since they are already spirit in their form and not limited with the physical weaknesses. Often people are sleeping at night, but Christians must learn to watch at night. One human spirit after another visited us, some with a friendly intent; some were enemies. At the time of our prayer, we again managed to have consistent prayer/spiritual warfare, so that our voices got loud and the ordinary people outside were wondering, for it was the first time that they encountered such people in their place. After we were exposed to that kind of reaction from people, we still continued our every night prayer, only that we lessened our voices so as to avoid trouble from the outside.

New things happened to us in our stay at Bay Laguna, both good and bad, yet God caused all of them to work together for good for those that love him. One of those things was, we were invited by a group of church leaders from Tayabas Quezon to train them, since they decided to get out of their former spiritually dead church. We once conducted a night of revival there (the video of this revival night was uploaded to Facebook, and to my surprise, I was greatly criticized and insulted by many, even Christians!), and that was three hours of preaching, worshipping, deliverance, and baptism of the Holy Spirit. The end part of this revival was being recorded into a video, and this lasted for at least eight minutes, and I happened to upload it, and church people had different reactions to that - both good and bad. That group of people decided to join us in our spiritual walk with the Lord as they faithfully obeyed him right after the Lord revived them, and instructed them to get out of their former church. Some of them were even shown a vision of Jesus standing at the outside of that church, at the door (like in Laodicea in Revelation 3:20-21), while the rest received a word and a dream. They decided to obey the Lord in getting out of their church, in spite of the persecutions and false accusations that they received from their leader and former church members; the fire of God in them couldn't be quenched by the physical hardships that they were experiencing. Now, they managed to gather a little number of faithful ones in that place, and even built a little chapel there. The Lord was more pleased with these little ones than that church that was large in number, yet was unfaithful to him.

Another change happened when prophetess (our mom) went to Saudi to work abroad. This made me at first to struggle since she was useful in our ministry as an inquirer; yet in this God had a plan. Her work made us little by little provide our material needs, since her commitment to that work was to provide for the church, she kept nothing from her own salary, but decided to send it all to us. Her first year at Saudi was a bit too difficult for her, since her first employer used to overwork her, and that often made her impatient. She was there without a cellphone, and we were only able to call once a month, and this lasted for almost a year. Then she managed to find another employer, and this made her able to have freedom to communicate to us; she happened to meet people through messenger and Facebook that were an instrument of the Lord to give us the next step of the ministry, the live streaming ministry.

The live streaming preaching ministry

Acts 16:9-10: *And a vision appeared to Paul in the night; There stood a man of Macedonia, and prayed him, saying, Come over into Macedonia, and help us. And after he had seen the vision, immediately we endeavoured to go into Macedonia, assuredly gathering that the Lord had called us for to preach the gospel unto them.*

While we were still at Bay Laguna, words of encouragement through a vision, dream and prophecy both from our members and from the brethren outside came unto us declaring the plan of God of expanding our tent ministry. One prophet said to me that the Lord showed him in a vision that he would provide women to help me begin this expansion of ministry, which later became the live streaming ministry preaching on Facebook. My mom was led to join a Christian chat group on messenger, and she added me into this. I was known to be a pastor by them, and there were pastors also there, which later went out one by one. I used to handle a Bible study in that group chat, and then suddenly we built a strong godly relationship in that group chat. It went on for months, then suddenly women in that group chat who were overseas Filipino workers (OFWs) in the Middle East, asked me to have an online preaching/teaching ministry. I told them that I liked that idea, yet I wasn't able to since we had no internet at our house. They promised to send me money that I would be able to have my internet. This seemed a big step, and at that time I was wondering still on the things that had happened. I later found out that this was the Lord's act.

At first, we began our live streaming ministry on an FM radio station. Yet, because of jealousy and misunderstanding, this ministry didn't last, and we transferred to the Facebook live streaming, up until now. This new step of faith, this expansion of ministry, made me to become like a kid that tries to learn to swim. At first, I was filled with excitement, and at the same time I was wondering where this one will lead me; often our earthly mind is ignorant of the things of the spirit. That is why it really needs to be renewed. At first, I used to preach using our Filipino language, and we had our Filipino people (most are OFWs) as our regular viewers. Some of the women that were used by God to begin this ministry also helped me promote the program, and this made the way for us to even reach the foreign brethren from different countries. When foreign believers began to follow our live streaming ministry, I was challenged and moved to make it using the English language, since they couldn't understand the Filipino language, and this caused me to struggle at first. I remember one time, years had passed by since the Holy Spirit had told me to study to use the English language. In my ignorance I tend to ignore the Lord's instructions, out of doubt, and was just thinking, "I don't need to study to speak the English language, since all of our church members are Filipino." Now, each time I was reminded of this instruction that I doubted at first, I only was able to hear the Lord telling me, "I told you". Our live streaming is in its first year and two months at the time that I am writing this book. It seems like it just happened yesterday. I praise God for his wisdom and powerful ability to fulfill all of his promises at the right time, and at the right place.

Fall away soldiers

2 Timothy 4:10: *For Demas hath forsaken me, having loved this present world, and is departed unto Thessalonica; Crescens to Galatia, Titus unto Dalmatia.*

John 6:66: *From that time many of his disciples went back, and walked no more with him.*

In our ministry people will come, and stay for a while, and go. There are some who stay for good, and there are some who stayed for a season, and some who came having a wrong motive, and some who stay because of Jesus. Nevertheless, we are to focus our life on serving the Lord until the end.

Even from Los Banos to Calamba, and Calamba to Bay, and now Bay to Los Banos again, Satan and his demons used to pursue us, trying to find a way to destroy us, even to stop us from spreading the gospel. Having this, we met different kinds of people along the way; people that stayed, and people that went away. Whatsoever the real motive is, these people can only stay with us for good because of Jesus, and would go away from us because of Jesus also. Among those people that stayed with us are the faithful viewers that were blessed by the Lord through our live streaming ministry, and likewise those who went out from us were deceived by the enemy, like others. The Lord led me to ask our people that stayed with us to write down their testimonies of how the Lord blessed them through our live streaming ministry. In this I decided to ask at least three Filipinos, and two foreign brethren, and you will see their testimonies at the end of this book. As for those people that walked out from us, even after receiving spiritual blessings from us, and us receiving a financial help from them, they went that way simply because they didn't continue following the message of the Lord. They were being misled since they began to listen to their minds, and to the deceptive spirit from other so-called believers that used to entice them.

Two of these fallen away soldiers that walked out from us were women. They once were zealous in their desire to serve the Lord by faithfully following our live streaming ministry, even to support and share the programs with others. It happened when one of these two sisters that were based in Canada asked me to pray for her through a phone call (messenger). She said that she wanted to receive the gift of the Holy Spirit, even to speak in tongues. It happened when I prayed with her, it was morning here in the Philippines, and it was evening to her in Canada. We prayed together, and by faith I laid hands on her (faith knows no distance or time gap), and then she received the gift of tongues and began to speak it, as she got baptized by the power of the Holy Spirit. We were excited then, and also the other sister that later on followed her on her way to deception. That was just the first time that this woman and I talked, and she didn't call me again. Her deception began due to her negligence to read the Bible. Aside from the gift of tongues, the Lord also allowed her to receive a gift of vision. Since I used to minister to our live streaming ministry followers daily, I wasn't able to talk to them for a while. Then suddenly, one day one of them shared to me a message that, according to them, was a revelation from God. When I asked about the message of revelation, she told me, "It's about the revelation of a prophet angel!" This sister was so excited when she said that to me. Then I began to ask her about this revelation, and where did she get that, or if she even had a Bible reference of it. Then she said, this revelation was given to her (the woman that I prayed for; her name was Bianca), and according to the Lord (the spirit that gave the revelation), she/Bianca is a prophet angel! This prophet angel, according to them, is that an individual human being like Bianca, is actually an angel here on earth! That she is just here as human, and will get out and return to her state of being an angel right after she finishes her mission. I was a little bit surprised by this, although I used to experience different kinds of false revelations from Satan given to different people in the church; some of them were the fallen away soldiers from our church. I gently and carefully gave my wise advice to this sister to ask Bianca to provide a scripture to back this revelation, even to prove whether this comes from God. Because in the Bible history, I only am aware of the story that took place where angels went into this world and took a human body so as to have a sexual relationship with women, and this was from the time of Jared to Noah (Genesis 5:18-32, 6:1-4), and those angels became fallen angels that were doomed to hell and were chained in the utter darkness of hell (Jude1:6, 2 Peter 2:4-5). Also, in Hebrews 13:2, and in some parts of Genesis, where people like Abraham happened to encounter angels, that according to many were in the human form, since they ate and drank with them (but to me, it was just a vision, since angels are not allowed to have a human body). Now, this sister tried to talk to Bianca at first, but Bianca (or the spirit in her) refused to provide biblical evidence for this revelation, and suddenly began to attack me, and even said to this sister to stop following me, or to not listen to my messages, since I was deceived. I tried to personally talk to Bianca, yet she refused to talk to me. Both of them went on their way, and I found out that they began following one of the false prophets here in the Philippines that had the name "Lobo". I even was told by one of our sisters (not a member of our church) that is a friend to Bianca that this prophet was telling them to go away from us, for we are deceived, and that he was asking them to give him three hundred thousand (300,000) pesos to invest in his business! The sister that told me about this, a friend of Bianca, tried to warn them to stop following such a kind of minister that was manipulating them to give him that large sum of money, but her efforts fell to nothing. These two sisters seemed like they were totally hypnotized by that kind of false prophet. The Lord also allowed me to hear from other brethren that they, too, were invited by these two sisters to follow this prophet, and afterward were asked to give him money. Now, I heard that these two sisters already went home to the Philippines and now were at the place of this prophet "Lobo", trying to blindly follow him. I felt sad about this. Due to the stubbornness of God's people, even the gifted were fallen victim to Satan, even after receiving the grace of power from God. When a little lamb gets out from the flock, being led by the good Shepherd, the danger is sure; death shall be the result of it.

If one will go away, another will come to fill in their position in the rank. God still is always in full control of everything. The people that the Lord sends into our rank are much more dedicated and passionate, and are willing to follow us, as we follow the Lord Jesus. They are coming one after another. They are coming the moment we needed them, because they came from God, who sends us into this battle field; he will not forsake his people, and he is fighting with them.

From Bay to Los Banos again

Matthew13:10-13:   *And the disciples came, and said unto him, Why speakest thou unto them in parables? He answered and said unto them, Because it is given unto you to know the mysteries of the kingdom of heaven, but to them it is not given. For whosoever hath, to him shall be given, and he shall have more abundance: but whosoever hath not, from him shall be taken away even that he hath. Therefore speak I to them in parables: because they seeing see not; and hearing they hear not, neither do they understand.*

Exactly one year after we moved to Bay, the Lord moved us again to our new target place, and we moved back to Los Banos. Having the new ministry that he entrusted to us, this live streaming ministry, God also blessed us with more wisdom and revelations to understand his word thoroughly. One of the blessings that the Lord gave to us that amazed me was the interpretation of the book of Revelation. While I was in the Bible school, I loved to stay at the library, because in that place I saw books! Books are the container of human knowledge and wisdom. Likewise, Christian books are believer's containers of their wisdom and revelations from God, and for some of course, just their man-made point of view. In that place I saw hundreds of different commentaries about the book of Revelation. Some were just the copy paste of others' work; some were just new discoveries. Each and every comment, and interpretations done by authors, can be a guidance to see the future, and in that case it's quite confusing to read hundreds of different interpretations. That also would mean hundreds of ways to see the future. God led me to study the book of Revelation even while I was in the Bible school, when I began our church's study, (that I did, thoroughly) and even until now. Because of that we managed to make an exposition of the book of Revelation daily to our live streaming ministry. Our interpretation of the book of Revelation is just the result of the Lord's wisdom, revelations, and our passionate desire to study the book (wisdom, and insights are being given to me one after another daily. Truly as we seek him, we will find him). People may easily disagree with the interpretations we gave in that exposition, simply because it's different from what has been taught to them in their church, or from their favorite theologian, yet unless one would study thoroughly without prejudice, they will begin to see things that they are supposed to see.

At the first two months of our stay at Los Banos, I was going hard about the live streaming, so that I did it twice a day! Every morning we did morning devotion, and then at night we preached spiritual warfare. Then we began the exposition of the book of Revelation at noon, then we taught spiritual warfare in the evening, and because of this, my physical condition went bad. The Lord gently advised me to take care of my body, and made me to just do our live steaming once a day. We tried to catch up into the new settings of our lives as servants, and as family members. I used to study during my spare time, then took care of our kids, then for a time tried to talk to our brethren (through messenger) that used to ask questions concerning doctrines, their family relationships, etc. In addition to this, I was attacked by the enemy using the false brethren trying to destroy me and the work of the Lord. Some of them were pretending pastors and believers that were being exposed every time we dealt with the deception of Satan being entertained by them. They were threatened and were angry toward us and began to falsely accuse us and malign us simply because they didn't want to hear us again; yet GREATER IS HE THAT IS IN ME, THAN HE THAT IS IN THEM! Their evil works didn't last for long, and they were gone, and by the grace of God I am still here faithfully doing the will of God. If new workers would come and go, likewise, our enemies would come and go. Like what happened to the disciples, every time they travelled to another place, Satan sent an enemy to attack them there (different enemy, different attacks in each and every place), yet God is powerful enough to defend his people. As long as we are doing God's will, and we follow his ways, we are protected.

The book: Jesus' Beginning

Isaiah 30:8: *Now go, write it before them in a table, and note it in a book, that it may be for the time to come forever and ever:*

Just before we transferred to Calamba from Los Banos, the Lord instructed us to carefully write in detail all the revelations and the spiritual encounters he gave to us, even the spiritual warfare. In obedience to God's word we did it, and after we almost finished it, we were thinking that it will be published soon. Yet God had something in his mind that we later understood through our experience. The testimonies were recorded as a book, and it took about five years (2013-2018) before it was again reviewed and re-written. Since some of the characters from the first testimonies were already gone from us, and changes happened that were from God, the book and its characters were refined through the fire, so that it had to go through many trials and testings just before the Lord would allow it to be published. Some of our people already lost their confidence about the book, so that they almost forgot it; but not the Lord! He knows better than we know. After a year of our live streaming ministry, I happened to have a gospel interview with pastor Eagle Sam (at Facebook Live), and that interview was uploaded at YouTube; it was entitled, *"From misery to ministry"*. Then one of our sisters that follows our live streaming ministry, sister Cheryl Fricke by name, told me to write down my testimony, for many shall be blessed upon the hearing of it, for the glory of the Lord. This surprised me, although I'd never given up on the book, suddenly God mentioned it again through this situation, and we know that nothing is a coincidence to the Lord. We talked through messenger, and I agreed to write the book. That call happened in the last week of March 2018, if I have not mistaken the date. Then this made me glad, and I shared the good news to our people. Some were happy, the others had no response, but nevertheless I treasured this in my heart. One of my dilemmas was that we lost the copy of the first record of our testimony, but the Lord comforted me by saying, "I will put into your remembrance everything that I told you(the revelations and the encounters)."I shared this word to prophetess (mom) who was at that time still working in Saudi, and was about to go back home in the month of June. We prayed to God for an instruction of when we would again begin to write the book, and he (God spoke through her) said, "Three months from the time that the instruction was given (March 23, 2018), you are to begin writing the book." Exactly at the time given by the Lord, we began to write the book at the first week of July 2018, and at this time we included the new testimonies from the new members of the church, and from our foreign brethren outside the country that followed our live streaming ministry. All the dilemmas were met one by one, and the word of the Lord stands above all. I give my highest praise to the One and Almighty God in the name of Jesus for this book! This book is so precious that it was written by the Lord in heaven, and was passed on into the earth so as to be read by men.

Audible voice of the Lord

1 Samuel 3:2: *And it came to pass at that time, when Eli was laid down in his place, and his eyes began to wax dim, that he could not see; And ere the lamp of God went out in the temple of the LORD, where the ark of God was, and Samuel was laid down to sleep; That the LORD called Samuel: and he answered, Here am I. And he ran unto Eli, and said, Here am I; for thou calledst me. And he said, I called not; lie down again. And he went and lay down. And the LORD called yet again, Samuel. And Samuel arose and went to Eli, and said, Here am I; for thou didst call me. And he answered, I called not, my son; lie down again. Now Samuel did not yet know the LORD, neither was the word of the LORD yet revealed unto him. And the LORD called Samuel again the third time. And he arose and went to Eli, and said, Here am I; for thou*

didst call me. And Eli perceived that the LORD had called the child. Therefore Eli said unto Samuel, Go, lie down: and it shall be, if he call thee, that thou shalt say, Speak, LORD; for thy servant heareth. So Samuel went and lay down in his place. And the LORD came, and stood, and called as at other times, Samuel, Samuel. Then Samuel answered, Speak; for thy servant heareth.

Acts 9:3-7: *And as he journeyed, he came near Damascus: and suddenly there shined round about him a light from heaven: And he fell to the earth, and heard a voice saying unto him, Saul, Saul, why persecutest thou me? And he said, Who art thou, Lord? And the Lord said, I am Jesus whom thou persecutest: it is hard for thee to kick against the pricks. And he trembling and astonished said, Lord, what wilt thou have me to do? And the Lord said unto him, Arise, and go into the city, and it shall be told thee what thou must do. And the men which journeyed with him stood speechless, hearing a voice, but seeing no man.*

One of the abilities that the Lord gave to the prophets of old and even to those in the New Testament was to hear him audibly. Although some traditional Christians, even ministers, doubt if this ability is still active nowadays, yet I will say, that this is still happening and can be experienced by those that the Lord chooses to stand before him in service. In our church the Lord opened our spiritual ears in various ways, and according to the measure of our faith. My mom, my brother, my wife, my niece and some members of our church had their ears opened by the Lord.

Exposing lies by hearing the Lord audibly

There was a situation when a woman visited us and asked us if she could stay with us for a time while she was looking for a place in which she could stay. This happened at Sucol Calamba, and this woman was a sister of my wife's friend Analyn. Then this woman began her work at Los Banos as a sales lady, and used to go home in the evening (seven p.m.). Then suddenly it happened that she didn't come home for a couple of nights, and when I asked her about this, she said that she happened to just a visit a friend and stayed in her house for a while, but the Lord told my niece (in an audible voice) that she was lying, and that she actually had a drinking party throughout the nights that she didn't come home, and that she stayed at her boyfriend's house (she is married). The Lord led me to confront her gently to confirm this, and then she admitted it, and asked for forgiveness for what she had done. The Lord forgave her, and then later on she decided to go home to her place at Cebu. I remember how God exposed Ananias' and Sapphira's lies, but sadly they failed to repent of it and were punished by the Lord with physical death. God wants to preserve the holiness of his house. He doesn't want any sin to hide and live in it, and so little by little corrupt the church. Praise God for the gift of hearing him through an audible voice.

This gift is really useful to us so as to expose Satan's demonic acts, and also to know something from the Lord. Through this gift, I was able to inquire of the Lord of certain things, and to receive specific instructions.

The effect of the gift to the receiver

Jeremiah 20:9: *Then I said, I will not make mention of him, nor speak any more in his name. But his word was in mine heart as a burning fire shut up in my bones, and I was weary with forbearing, and I could not stay.*

Through our daily experiences of receiving power and gifts from the Lord, we little by little understand the life of the prophets, even from the Old Testament. People can't easily understand the things of the Spirit unless they experience them. According to the recipient of the gift, when they begin to operate in it, it seemed likely that they were transferred to a different dimension. Physically I can talk to them, yet their Spirit is present in another dimension, that it sometimes made them difficult to focus. They said that the experience was like a person that swims deeply into the sea; the deeper it gets, the harder it is! Yet every great treasure of the kingdom can only be found in the deepest part of the Spirit/sea. Sometimes they were hurting every time they tried to receive an answer from the Lord, and sometimes their body would bear the pressure. There were different physical reactions from them every time they began to enter into the spiritual realm, and sometimes they would get hurt by the enemies in the spirit, so that they could vividly feel the pain in their physical bodies. Sometimes if their faith was not enough, I had to lay my hands on them to pour out fire on them to empower them in the name of Jesus so that they would be able to go into the spiritual world and see things in it and share it with us afterward.

Spiritual gifts and power

1 Corinthians 12:4-11: *Now there are diversities of gifts, but the same Spirit. And there are differences of administrations, but the same Lord. And there are diversities of operations, but it is the*

same God which worketh all in all. But the manifestation of the Spirit is given to every man to profit withal. For to one is given by the Spirit the word of wisdom; to another the word of knowledge by the same Spirit; To another faith by the same Spirit; to another the gifts of healing by the same Spirit; To another the working of miracles; to another prophecy; to another discerning of spirits; to another divers kinds of tongues; to another the interpretation of tongues: But all these worketh that one and the selfsame Spirit, dividing to every man severally as he will.

As we are seeking, God provides. As we earnestly seek God's presence and want to offer him a worship that he deserves (John 4:23-24) God led us into himself so as to experience his power and presence. It is only by the power of the Holy Spirit that we can worship God the way that is acceptable to him, and in this, spiritual gifts and power are required. God is a God of order, and out of love we want to really satisfy him with all that we have by the grace of the Spirit. In having the experiences of worshipping God in different churches I saw two kinds of worship being offered to him: dead and alive worship. In this we seek to offer him a living sacrifice. Since we decided to follow him, we are determined to really please him.

Worship is the same as service; that's why in Romans 12:1 it says, *I beseech you therefore, brethren, by the mercies of God, that ye present your bodies a living sacrifice, holy, acceptable unto God, which is your reasonable service.*

God is expecting for a reasonable or a spiritual service on our behalf. Sadly, many are blind and deaf to this truth, making their gathering together a gathering of living dead Christians. God from time to time blesses us, his church, with gifts and power, and by his grace I will try to explain each and every one of these gifts and power, their effect, how Satan counterfeited them, and how we can be able to resist this evil work of twisting the gifts and power of God.

The fivefold ministry

Ephesians 4:11: *And he gave some, apostles; and some, prophets; and some, evangelists; and some, pastors and teachers;*

1 Peter 4:10-11: *As every man hath received the gift, even so minister the same one to another, as good stewards of the manifold grace of God. If any man speak, let him speak as the oracles of God; if any man minister, let him do it as of the ability which God giveth: that God in all things may be glorified through Jesus Christ, to whom be praise and dominion forever and ever. Amen.*

When a man or a woman decides to go into full-time ministry, often they will be called a pastor. Yet in the ministry, we have to understand that there are different ministries that God designed for each and every one that went up into a pulpit to preach. With the listed passages above, we will see that there are five ministries that every full-time minister could have, and that they ought to find the right one and spend their lifetime there. Unless ministers find and do their specific jobs (Ephesians 4:11) they can never experience God's fullness of blessings; they will end up only having an average service to the Lord. Often this leads to spiritual dryness, and to some it will be an untimely death.

Gifts, effects, and ministry

Apostles: Jesus had twelve disciples, but not all of them were apostles. Phillip was called an evangelist, and Andrew seems likely to have been an evangelist too, for he often led people to Christ. An apostle is the one that is being used by God to preach and teach the gospel in order to establish churches. They will be the one to establish its foundation, and build up its leadership, until the time shall come that they can stand alone, and thereby the apostle will leave them so as to find another place to begin establishing a church. Often, they are called church planters. They are blessed with power such as signs and wonders, miracles, prophecy, and authority over the church they established, like what we read about Paul and Peter.

Prophets: There were prophets in the Old Testament, and there were prophets in the New Testament, and there still are even now. The work of the prophet often is in prophecy; to declare the message that has to do with the future. They also are in the preaching and teaching ministry, and also can be the leader of a church (often they are called "pastor" to begin with). In the Old Testament they are called "a seer" - the eye, ear, and mouthpiece of God. They also can be blessed with the power to perform healing, signs and wonders, and miracles, yet mostly they are in prophecy, and compared to the apostle, they can be just at one place. They will move only so as to do a specific mission such as to give a word to a specific person, yet after that they again will go back to their place. I also found out by the grace of God that each and everyone has their bestowed mission from God. Moses, for example, was given the mission to deliver Israel from Egypt, Samuel to lead them until they asked for a king. Elijah was used to revive them at the time of their apostasy, and Elisha received a double power to restore what was being stolen away from them by their enemies. Silas was a prophet to accompany Paul in his journey.

Evangelists: Andrew, Phillip, and the Samaritan woman were just a few of the people that had the ministry of evangelism. To evangelize a person means you are drawing him or her near to Christ. It doesn't matter whether you are the one that is preaching or teaching the gospel. Evangelists are given the power to persuade the person to believe in Christ up to the point of meeting him in person. Andrew ushered Peter to Christ (John 1:41-42). Phillip led Nathaniel and the eunuch to Christ (John 1:45, Acts 8:29-40), and the Samaritan woman led her people to him (John 4:28-30). They also had been given the power to perform signs and wonders, miracles, and healing.

Pastors: These are those that have been entrusted with the ability and the power to take care of the flocks. They often were given the compassion and the heart to watch over them until they come up to spiritual maturity, enough to lead others. There is a confusing manmade idea that used to spread out throughout the churches that forbid women to be a pastor, so as to lead the church. They back up their claim only with 1 Timothy 2:12, without knowing that the passage was just the issue about husband and wife. I often dealt with this topic in my messages, yet people, once having been framed by a teaching, find it very hard to get out of it, unless they have an open heart and mind so as to listen for a deeper understanding. Even after providing evidence both in the scriptures and in reality, they still will close their mind to it, therefore it's useless to talk to them. They end up becoming a follower of those who just listen to their own minds, and not to the mind of God. The truth of women leading the church so as to preach (1 Timothy 2:12 only deals with teaching) and to teach is quite clear both in the Old Testament and in the New Testament. Miriam was a prophetess (Exodus 15:20), Deborah led Israel to the battle (Judges 4:4), Huldah was being sought for counsel by the priest and the noble men (2Kings 22:14), and in the New Testament, Anna was a prophetess (Luke 2:36). The word "elder" in 1 Timothy 5:17, is "presbuteros" in the Greek. Both men and women used to pastor the church at the time of Paul. The calling of God on a person can't be bound by human tradition, age, or gender, because it is spiritual in nature. By evidence, we know women in the ministry that were/are used by God to draw multitudes of people to him; therefore, if God doesn't approve of this service of women, why would he bless them?

Teachers: Jesus possesses all these gifts, and gave them to the church (Ephesians 4:9-11) according to the measure of his grace, so one can receive from God. A teacher is to be in the office of teaching ministry so to nurture the church in their spiritual life that they may grow in their knowledge of the Lord. Each minister can teach; however, with a limited portion of teaching. Apollo was a teacher. Paul said, "I planted, and Apollo watered (1 Corinthians 3:6)". To water is to continue blessing the soil that received the seed of faith.   The Corinthian people in their ignorance unintentionally compared Paul's work to Apollo's and Peter's, yet he gently rebuked them by teaching of the difference of their work, and that they are not that important, because God is the one that is causing the growth. The teaching ministry is to educate the church of our faith in Christ, and they are there to explain things they should know. We know that the church perishes because of lack of knowledge. It is because of the lack of the growth in knowledge that we often become stagnant and unfruitful, which is what had happened with the Corinthian and Hebrew believers. Mostly teachers have their own Bible school. The teaching ministry helps the believers grow in the knowledge of the Lord so that they don't have to drink milk at a time that they ought to be eating meat! And, so that they can teach others at the right time, and not have themselves be taught again, which hinders the progress of evangelism.

The danger of going into a wrong ministry

Throughout the Old Testament and in the New Testament, people of God received a punishment from God due to their arrogance (and lack of knowledge) by trying to be in a ministry that did not belong to them. Below is a list of just some of them.

King Uzziah

2 Chronicles 26:16-21: *But when he was strong, his heart was lifted up to his destruction: for he transgressed against the LORD his God, and went into the temple of the LORD to burn incense upon the altar of incense. And Azariah the priest went in after him, and with him fourscore priests of the LORD, that were valiant men: And they withstood Uzziah the king, and said unto him, It appertaineth not unto thee, Uzziah, to burn incense unto the LORD, but to the priests the sons of Aaron, that are consecrated to burn incense: go out of the sanctuary; for thou hast trespassed; neither shall it be for thine honour from the LORD God. Then Uzziah was wroth, and had a censer in his hand to burn incense: and while he was wroth with the priests, the leprosy even rose up in his forehead before the priests in the house of the LORD, from beside the incense altar. And Azariah the chief priest, and all the priests, looked upon him, and, behold, he was leprous in his forehead, and they thrust him out from thence; yea, himself hasted also to go out, because the LORD had smitten him. And Uzziah the king was a leper unto the day of his death, and dwelt in a several house, being a leper; for he was cut off from the house of the LORD: and Jotham his son was over the king's house, judging the people of the land.*

Miriam and Aaron

Numbers 12:8-11: *With him will I speak mouth to mouth, even apparently, and not in dark speeches; and the similitude of the LORD shall he behold: wherefore then were ye not afraid to speak against my servant Moses?   And the anger of the LORD was kindled against them; and he departed.   And the cloud departed from off the tabernacle; and, behold, Miriam became leprous, white as snow: and Aaron looked upon Miriam, and, behold, she was leprous. And Aaron said unto Moses, Alas, my lord, I beseech thee, lay not the sin upon us, wherein we have done foolishly, and wherein we have sinned.*

Korah, Dathan, and Abiram

Numbers 16:1-4: *Now Korah, the son of Izhar, the son of Kohath, the son of Levi, and Dathan and Abiram, the sons of Eliab, and On, the son of Peleth, sons of Reuben, took men: And they rose up before Moses, with certain of the children of Israel, two hundred and fifty princes of the assembly, famous in the congregation, men of renown: And they gathered themselves together against Moses and against Aaron, and said unto them, Ye take too much upon you, seeing all the congregation are holy, every one of them, and the LORD is among them: wherefore then lift ye up yourselves above the congregation of the LORD?   And when Moses heard it, he fell upon his face:*

Numbers 16:28-35: *And Moses said, Hereby ye shall know that the LORD hath sent me to do all these works; for I have not done them of mine own mind. If these men die the common death of all men, or if they be visited after the visitation of all men; then the LORD hath not sent me.   But if the LORD make a new thing, and the earth open her mouth, and swallow them up, with all that appertain unto them, and they go down quick into the pit; then ye shall understand that these men have provoked the LORD.   And it came to pass, as he had made an end of speaking all these words, that the ground clave asunder that was under them: And the earth opened her mouth, and swallowed them up, and their houses, and all the men that appertained unto Korah, and all their goods. They, and all that appertained to them, went down alive into the pit, and the earth closed upon them: and they perished from among the congregation. And all Israel that were round about them fled at the cry of them: for they said, Lest the earth swallow us up also. And there came out a fire from the LORD, and consumed the two hundred and fifty men that offered incense.*

In the New Testament these people often fell into the category of being false apostles, false teachers, and antichrists. The apostles used to warn the church against them, even to mention the name of some of them.

Untimely death as a result of this sin

We hear of pastors that die in a plane crash, car accident, ship that sank, and so on. December 30, 2013, we had five pastors that died here in the Philippines, and one of them was a bishop. They died in a car accident; their van went onto the wrong side of the road and so hit the bus before them. The police report said that the driver went to sleep while driving, since they came from Tacloban Leyte after giving relief goods to the victims of a super typhoon. One may ask, "What went wrong? Why did it happen?" Since the death of the Lord's servant is precious to him (Psalm 116:15), does that include dying in that untimely death? Sometimes when things go wrong, we fail to seek for an answer from the Lord. When we ask, surely the Lord will answer, but when he provides the answer, are you ready to receive it? Things like the incident above happen one time after another in different places and different times all over the world, and they are happening to his servants who are precious to him. When we inquired of the Lord (for I will not stop pursuing things until I receive enlightenment) about these things that took place among his servants, these accidents that took their lives, the Lord gently yet firmly answered us with a shaking revelation; he said, "That happened to them because of their stubbornness! They kept on doing things that I didn't ask them to do. They are doing the ministry that I never told them to do. It's just their own will, their own minds, and I'd never be pleased with that kind of service. Many were being misled and so perished because of that kind of misleading ministry. One must not do things without my consent. I am the Lord; you should honor me and not yourself!" The Lord went on saying, "If one would do a ministry apart from my will, there will be a disastrous effect of it on my people, and Satan will interfere, and they will become his servants, destroying my people's faith instead of edifying them. When one would try to be a teacher without the anointing of the Holy Spirit, what would take place is the counterfeit power of Satan to manifest in that ministry, and the result will be disastrous! How many among them live in this way, that after so many warnings that I sent to them, they still fail to repent and stubbornly go on their misleading ways, misleading many; and they boast of it, and my blind people praise them! Yet in my holiness I no longer will tolerate this kind of evil work in my vineyard. If you want to serve me and become useful to me, you have to fully surrender all of your mind, emotion, spirit, and body to me. For that is the only way that I can use you fully and make you a blessing to many. Many were just able to serve me half-heartedly, so that I couldn't move in them fully, since their will is too strong against me! I don't force myself on anyone. I want total surrender of oneself to my hand so that I can fill them of myself. The spirit is willing, yet the flesh is weak, and often they fail to obey the Spirit since they listen to their fleshly desires rather than to the desires of the Spirit, and this made them to die untimely. If a person would serve me, he or she must sit first and evaluate the cost of following me (Luke 14:26-30), otherwise it only will end in failure."

I wonder how many ministers belittle the cost of discipleship. They speak out things that they do not know and lead others to do the same. Motives are different as to why they speak foolish things such as this. Some impart to others their failure to lay down everything to Jesus. They will even try to back it up with the scriptures, even to twist its meaning just to back up their evil intentions. Nevertheless, the Lord is not sleeping. He will judge his people, and will purify them, and will remove from them the wicked one.

In regard to the false teachings about the second coming

2 Thessalonians 2:1-3: *Now we beseech you, brethren, by the coming of our Lord Jesus Christ, and by our gathering together unto him, That ye be not soon shaken in mind, or be troubled, neither by spirit, nor by word, nor by letter as from us, as that the day of Christ is at hand. Let no man deceive you by any means: for that day shall not come, except there come a falling away first, and that man of sin be revealed, the son of perdition;*

2 Peter 3:3-4: *Knowing this first, that there shall come in the last days scoffers, walking after their own lusts, And saying, Where is the promise of his coming? for since the fathers fell asleep, all things continue as they were from the beginning of the creation.*

We decided to discuss about some false teachings here that are relevant to our lives as end-times saints. One of the false teachings that has deceived our people throughout many churches is the false concept of the second coming of the Lord. Even from the time of the apostles Satan sent wolves in sheep's clothing so as to twist this message to them, so that they would lose their hope in Jesus. Since early Christians were greatly persecuted by the Roman empire, the Lord strengthened their faith by the message of the second coming. Since their lives were always on the edge of the sword, the apostles were led by the Spirit to make them forget their lives on earth by fixing their hope in heaven from which the coming Savior would appear (Titus 2:13) to reward the faithful and to render punishment to the unfaithful. Satan tried to twist the message of the coming of the Lord by telling people it had already happened (2 Thessalonians 2:1), that the church was waiting for nothing. Yet the Lord empowered them by abolishing this kind of false teaching, moving the apostles to direct them into the truth, so as to provide a sign of the end times; the coming of the man of sin and his appearance in the place so as to proclaim himself to be God, the place in which only the high priest was allowed, the holy of holies (2 Thessalonians 2:3-7). The rapture of the church should take place first, for unless it happens, the Holy Spirit that restrains the antichrist/man of sin will not be taken away (together with the church, verses 5-7). Peter was battling different false teachings of the end times from the people that caused doubt among the believers. Those false teachers (2 Peter chapter 3:4) say, *"Where is the promise of his coming? for since the fathers fell asleep, all things continue as they were from the beginning of the creation."* Yet the apostle firmly establishes the faith of the church by the word of faithfulness that was given to them by the Holy Spirit. Peter reminded them that the word of God is faithful enough to create everything, and to destroy everything by the flood, and also by the fire, only to exchange it with the glorious one.

Nowadays churches fail to understand the importance of the message of the second coming to the heart of the believers. They focus too much on the message of prosperity in terms of material things, which later on makes them deny their faith in Christ. There are many reasons people of God nowadays lack the interest of knowing the signs of the coming of the Lord. The leaders seem like they are sleeping so as to not know of this. The footsteps of the martyred seem like they are being erased by the false teachers, and many are not aware of this, and many don't care to know this. Yet, we are here, appointed by God, to once again get the church back into the footsteps of the martyred disciples, that first followed the footsteps of Christ, while carrying the cross that Christ gave us.

About resurrection

2 Timothy 2:17-18: *And their word will eat as doth a canker: of whom is Hymenaeus and Philetus; Who concerning the truth have erred, saying that the resurrection is past already; and overthrow the faith of some.*

1 Timothy 1:19-20: *Holding faith, and a good conscience; which some having put away concerning faith have made shipwreck: Of whom is Hymenaeus and Alexander; whom I have delivered unto Satan, that they may learn not to blaspheme.*

Even ministers and churches are not in agreement as to the teaching of resurrection. I encountered some of them who are not that sure of the belief in regard to this blessed hope of Christianity. I wonder how churches can disregard the most important part of the gospel, in which the disciples of Christ put much emphasis on in their writing, since according to them, it is the final end of everything. Some of our people were just careless enough to not study thoroughly this message that was often taught to the early Christians by the faithful apostles. This I believe was one of the main factors as to why Christianity nowadays lacks power - simply because they no longer take heed to the message of the gospel that has to do with the resurrection. In the New Testament there are three words used for resurrection to describe the event.

Anastasis (Matthew 22:23): This is the standing up again (literally) from the dead. This one emphasizes the truth of life after death in heaven.

The idea of this resurrection is the place of life after death. When the Sadducees tried to test Jesus' wisdom, they gave him a story of a woman who had seven husbands while still living in this world, and all of the husbands died one after another, and finally the woman died. Following their presumptuous idea (that there is no resurrection), they asked Jesus, in heaven whose wife will she be, since she had the seven of them here on earth? Jesus simply corrected their error about resurrection and told them that in the resurrection, or in the life after death in this world, we will not do things like we did here on earth; like the sexual relationship between the husband and wife; for we will live like angels. The idea of anastasis focuses on the place of life after death, not on the changing of our physical body to become a glorious one as egersis (below) tells us. It has to do with the kind of place that we will have just when we will be resurrected. That's why in John 5:28-29, Jesus mentioned the two places in which people can go in the afterlife; a place of damnation and a place of life (in heaven).

Egersis (Matthew 27:53): A resurgence.

This is the only record in the Bible that clearly tells us about the event of the saints that have been resurrected; they were raised up to life again into their physical body. Jesus was the first!

This event of resurrection is the rising up of the dead body to life (the union of the spirit to its dead physical body, since a body without a spirit is dead (James 2:26)) and it will later on have its glorious form at the second coming, as it is promised to the saints by the Lord. This is also the same as the resurrection that is mentioned in Revelation 20:4-6, the two events of physical resurrection. The first as we read in Matthew 27:53 took place right after Jesus' resurrection from the dead, since he is the first resurrected from the dead (1 Corinthians 15:20), and was followed by the saints (from the Old Testament) as the first batch/event of this by the changing of a physical body to a glorious one. The second event of this shall be at the second coming (1 Thessalonians 4:15-17). Though many have a different point of view on this subject, we decided to ask the Lord about it, and he opened our minds to it so as to gain an understanding of the subject.

Exanastasis (Philippians 3:11): A rising from the dead.

This kind of resurrection mentioned only by Paul in his letter to the Philippians, has to do with the "time" of catching or snatching away of our body in this world that will happen only at the second coming, so as to change us instantly (1 Corinthians 15:51-53) in the air, meeting the Lord in the air. It deals with the time or the schedule of the said subject. I believe this shall be the complete resurrection of our physical body so as to make it heavenly - spirit in substance.

So, the three resurrections in the New Testament deal with the place (anastasis), the actual (egersis), and the time (exanastasis) of the event.

In addition to this, about the actual event of resurrection, we can see the three kinds of this actual event that happened to different characters in the Bible.

First, the temporary resurrection of the physical body.

Jairus' daughter (Mark 5:35-43): In this event the daughter of Jairus was already declared physically dead (verse 35) - the same physical death that happened to Lazarus (John11:13-14), and to the son of the woman at Nain (Luke 7:12). These three people experienced the power of Jesus' resurrection temporarily. Literally they were raised back to life, yet it was just a temporary resurrection, since after that resurrection they still died in their physical bodies, and needed to experience egersis, the actual event of resurrection.

Second, the temporary resurrection of the spirit.

Ephesians 2:5: *Even when we were dead in sins, hath quickened us together with Christ, (by grace ye are saved;)*

This spiritual resurrection happens the moment an unbeliever, a spiritually dead person, repents of his sins, and surrenders his life to Jesus in response to the message of the gospel. The dead spirit becomes alive, and is born again by faith in Christ. This is just a temporary resurrection of the spirit, since a person that was once a believer and a follower of Jesus can still one day decide (though it is not the will of God) to turn his back on Jesus and go back to the life of sin, until such a time that he can never get back to Christ, and he dies in that state of disobedience. Though traditional Christians don't agree on this, there are many biblical references of this truth that we can find, such as Philippians 3:18-19, Hebrews 6:4-8, 10:26-31, John 15:2, John 15:6, 2 Peter 2:17-22, Revelation 3:5, and so on.

Third, the final resurrection (egersis).

1 Corinthians 15:51-55: *Behold, I show you a mystery; We shall not all sleep, but we shall all be changed, In a moment, in the twinkling of an eye, at the last trump: for the trumpet shall sound, and the dead shall be raised incorruptible, and we shall be changed. For this corruptible must put on incorruption, and this mortal must put on immortality. So when this corruptible shall have put on incorruption, and this mortal shall have put on immortality, then shall be brought to pass the saying that is written, Death is swallowed up in victory. O death, where is thy sting? O grave, where is thy victory?*

My personal testimony of the preacher that fell away from grace

2 Peter 2:1: *But there were false prophets also among the people, even as there shall be false teachers among you, who privily shall bring in damnable heresies, even denying the Lord that bought them, and bring upon themselves swift destruction. And many shall follow their pernicious ways; by reason of whom the way of truth shall be evil spoken of. And through covetousness shall they with feigned words make merchandise of you: whose judgment now of a long time lingereth not, and their damnation slumbereth not.*

I know a man that was famous for his teaching and preaching at the time when I was just a youth in the church, and even when he died, he still was famous. He died famous, and people believed that heaven received him simply because he had built a large ministry, he wrote and sold many books, and even became a well-known speaker, being invited by many churches all over the world. I even admired him at that time (due to my ignorance to discern the spirit/message). In June 2018, I learned that he and his wife died in a plane crash! I hadn't heard of him since the time that the Lord took me out of the crowd to be trained by him. I was surprised then upon the knowledge of his death. He was just fifty, too young to die. When I inquired of the Lord about the place of this man to spend his eternity, I was shaken when the Lord said that he is to spend it in hell! I asked, "Why, Lord?" then the Lord moved me to listen to his messages, and I found out why. He committed the sin of blasphemy against the Holy Spirit by teaching a different message than what is in the Bible. In his preaching he said that Jesus didn't preach about "born again, resurrection, and spiritual worship". He also once made fun of the blood of Jesus (see Hebrews 10:29). I also found out that this man was one that preached the prosperity gospel. In their message, they value money and material things rather than spirituality/living in the

Spirit. He now was reaping what he sowed in the flesh: corruption.

Many theologians, scholars, and ministers teach a misleading statement concerning the blasphemy against the Holy Spirit, that this only can be committed by the unbelievers, and not by the believers. Yet I will tell you "take heed if you think you are standing lest you fall!" You may back up your claims with the scriptures, and even with physical evidences, yet if it doesn't glorify Jesus, and only promotes the flesh, you are in a danger zone of falling away from the grace of God.

Blasphemy against the Holy Spirit can actually be committed both by unbelievers and believers. It is a direct contempt against the Spirit of God, by telling or making his work appear evil, and the work of Satan appear good.

Many don't want to believe that a believer can fall away from the grace of God. They misunderstand God's grace. They say that you are not a true believer if you will turn your back on Jesus. They deny man's freewill. They are biased by just picking up some verses and explaining them to verify their favorite dogmas. However, God isn't pleased with this kind of misjudgment. God wants his people to grow in their knowledge of him, and not in men. In a simple logical statement, "You can't fall away from grace if you haven't been there once," and also, you can't turn your back on Jesus you if you haven't once known him. That's why Peter strongly stated,

2 Peter 2:21: *For it had been better for them not to have known the way of righteousness, than, after they have known it, to turn from the holy commandment delivered unto them.*

And Paul,

Philippians 3:18-19: *(For many walk, of whom I have told you often, and now tell you even weeping, that they are the enemies of the cross of Christ: Whose end is destruction, whose God is their belly, and whose glory is in their shame, who mind earthly things.)*

Sin against the Holy Spirit (by Christians and non-Christians)

It was said that every sin done against Jesus can be forgiven, but every sin committed against the Holy Spirit can't be forgiven in this age, and in the age that is to come (Matthew12:31-32). It is an eternal sin that often is misunderstood by many who try to throw the blame only to the unbelievers. This sin can actually be committed by both unbelievers and believers. One may disagree with me, but the Bible shall be our basis of truth, not any human point of view. They said contextually it was the Pharisees that Jesus was talking about, yet the Pharisees were considered to be dead branches of the vine.

1 Thessalonians 5:19-20: *Quench not the Spirit. Despise not prophesyings.*

Quenching the Holy Spirit is either an act or a word made by us so as to stop the work of the Holy Spirit. It means to extinguish, like a fire that is killed by water or something. Often this is being done out of ignorance by the immature, and intentionally by the backsliders. How many people speak out hurting words against a group of believers that experience extraordinary things provided to them by the Holy Spirit? One example of this is when a person gets filled by the Holy Spirit's power, and suddenly his physical body starts shaking as if he is convulsing, in that they immediately conclude that it is a work of the devil. But I tell you that Jesus warned us not to judge outwardly (John 7:24).

Let me explain to you a little about those that shake their bodies and fall slain when they receive God's power. Based on the Bible and on our own experience, our bodies can't really contain God's power. It's only by the grace of God that he allows us to taste this power, and just to the point that our body will realize it. Once you experience the power of God, that is not something you can really explain with your limited mind, it's more in the Spirit, yet our physical reactions must not be the only basis of God's working, it still must be spiritual (for some try to mimic others, and do it by the flesh; this is evil). Even the falling of one's body on the floor is just the reaction, not the power itself. Yet we also must be cautious and stand up for Jesus, and not to stay fallen on the floor all day!

So, this sin of extinguishing the Spirit can be committed by those that don't allow the manifestations of spiritual gifts and power in their church, especially the gift of prophecy (1 Thessalonians 5:20). Traditional churches often fall into this error because of the misunderstanding of God's power. As Jesus said to the Pharisees in Mark 12:24: *And Jesus answering said unto them, Do ye not therefore err, because ye know not the scriptures, neither the power of God?*

Grieving the Holy Spirit

Ephesians 4:30: *And grieve not the holy Spirit of God, whereby ye are sealed unto the day of redemption.*

In Greek the word is "lupeo", and it means to be sorrowful, to cause grief or distress. In the context of Ephesians 4, it is more likely to speak out evil hurting words against one another. Once a believer speaks words that would damage the heart of the brethren, the Holy Spirit feels it the same way. How often Jesus tells us to be careful with our words, otherwise we will be accountable for them in the judgment day (Matthew 12:36-37). That is why we are told to forgive one another instead of to retaliate against others. How many churches go on bad-mouthing and fist-fighting every time there is a quarrel in them?   How sad it is to see us in this manner, without being aware of God watching us that moment.

Blasphemy against the Holy Spirit

Matthew 12:31-32: *Wherefore I say unto you, All manner of sin and blasphemy shall be forgiven unto men: but the blasphemy against the Holy Ghost shall not be forgiven unto men. And whosoever speaketh a word against the Son of man, it shall be forgiven him: but whosoever speaketh against the Holy Ghost, it shall not be forgiven him, neither in this world, neither in the world to come.*

Unforgivable sin, as others call it. In the passage above, Jesus refers to the Pharisees, yet now he is telling it to all of us. Pharisees were just being likened to a dead branch of the vine. And nowadays, they are the dead Christians who outwardly are alive, but inwardly are dead like the church of Sardis (Revelation 3:1). Outwardly they are rich and prosperous, but inwardly are wretched, and miserable, and poor, and blind, and naked, like the lukewarm Laodicean church. The way they live is contrary to the gospel of Jesus that leads people into the life of the Spirit by denying the desires of the flesh.

Understanding spirituality

Galatians 5:16-26: *This I say then, walk in the Spirit, and ye shall not fulfil the lust of the flesh. For the flesh lusteth against the Spirit, and the Spirit against the flesh: and these are contrary the one to the other: so that ye cannot do the things that ye would. But if ye be led of the Spirit, ye are not under the law. Now the works of the flesh are manifest, which are these; adultery, fornication, uncleanness, lasciviousness, idolatry, witchcraft, hatred, variance, emulations, wrath, strife, seditions, heresies, envyings, murders, drunkenness, revellings, and such like: of the which I tell you before, as I have also told you in time past, that they which do such things shall not inherit the kingdom of God. But the fruit of the Spirit is love, joy, peace, longsuffering, gentleness, goodness, faith, meekness, temperance: against such there is no law. And they that are Christ's have crucified the flesh with the affections and lusts. If we live in the Spirit, let us also walk in the Spirit. Let us not be desirous of vain glory, provoking one another, envying one another.*

Man's misery in this world began when sin entered into this world through Adam and Eve. Thereby all sin and all die, yet through Jesus Christ, God's righteousness was revealed by his sacrificial offering on the cross; it provides a new and a living way, and that is life in the Spirit. Jesus showed us the example of living a spiritual life here on earth, and that is by the power of the Holy Spirit; it is only by the abiding presence of the Spirit that we can be able to deny the works of the flesh.

I once was a drunkard, a gambler, a drug user, and used to get involved in fornication and things that made me to live in darkness. I praise God that he didn't let me die in that darkened life. When I decided to follow Jesus, his blood cleansed me from all the guilt of sin. Yet still, as long as we are in this world, we still can fall into Satan's snare. One thing the Lord assured me of, he will be my guide, my advocate and my helper so as to make me continue my journey with him, and this truth has made me to come this far, and I am even willing to go beyond, because I know that he is with me always.

Welcome to the spiritual realm

We, as human beings, believers and unbelievers alike, are living in two different dimensions, whether we accept it or not. We are spirits, in the flesh. Our flesh belongs to this world, yet our spirit belongs to the spirit realm. Christians are often ignorant of the spiritual realm, and this has made Satan take advantage of them in war. In the Bible there are many passages that help us understand about this truth, yet still many are doubtful. The difference between the early church and the now church is that they were more spiritually sensitive during their time than we are now. They were more prayerful in that they could gather every day without fail, even after the persecution of the Roman empire. They were unstoppable! They studied the scriptures daily, and preached the gospel as the Lord guided them. Therefore, he granted them to experience extraordinary miracles in a way that was just common to every one of them (see Acts 2:42-47).

The Lord blesses our church with gifts and power, and also extraordinary experiences, that to the immature seem impossible, but to the mature, all things are possible with God. I will try by the grace of God to list down the experiences, and even to put some of the personal testimonies of each member. From this point on, I ask you to please be prayerful enough to test the spirit first before you will make a judgment.

Opening of the spiritual eyes and ears

Job 42:5: *I have heard of thee by the hearing of the ear: but now mine eye seeth thee.*

When God began to open our spiritual eyes and ears, he first cleansed us from all impurities so as to prepare us for the encounter. As we gathered every night, God led us into the spiritual gradually. Some of our members were able to see the spiritual world in their visions as if they were just watching a movie, yet the experience was real, because when they were in the battle field and got hit by the enemy, they could feel it in their physical bodies (with the volume of pain that each could endure). They were able to see demons, and even hear them engaging to fight against them in the battle. This battle began just when we decided to gather (for Satan knows who will seriously attend the meeting, and even tries to discourage them from going; often many fell into this kind of deception). Satan will try to stop you from attending the fellowship in so many ways. Through the weather, people around you, sickness, etc.; yet every one that is determined to go will surely overcome them, if only they will use their discernment.

One of the blessings of having your spiritual eyes and ears being opened is that your understanding of the spiritual world will go deeper. Often ministers teach about the spiritual world through their knowledge of the Bible, and their own interpretations, and often they fall short of its reality. God, however, doesn't just want us to speak of these things (out of head knowledge), but also to experience them ourselves. The depth and height of this reality only depend on the grace of God. As long as we have the longing to have it, God will give it to us, since it is he who made us to seek for these things. Demons are very good at hiding, and they love to fool people into believing they don't exist. You may not be able to see them with your eyes now, but if you will try to see their evil works around you, you will begin to see the evidence of their existence. There are lots of people (like atheists) who don't believe in spirits. They use their futile human knowledge of just the physical creation. Even if you will try to present to them lots of evidence, still they will deny it, simply because they don't want to believe it, and they are not looking for the truth. If you are to look for a carpenter, and suddenly you behold the house he built, is it not the evidence that the carpenter exists?   Likewise, demons and angels are spirits that we can't simply see or discern with our physical senses, yet through the evil things that demons are doing and through our spiritual eyes and ears being opened, we can see them.   As spirit beings, they are much higher than humans in everything.   They are swift to move, tireless, eternal, and knowledgeable.   That is why the only way that Christians can defeat demons is through the power and wisdom of the Holy Spirit.

In comparison to God, angels and demons are limited in knowledge and power, and can't be omnipresent.   That's why when Satan tried to go up to the level of God, to be worshiped like God, he failed, simply because he lacks the divine attributes of God.   He has limitations as a created being, whereas the Creator has no limitations.

Talking to human spirits and presenting Jesus to them

Acts 16:9-10: *And a vision appeared to Paul in the night; There stood a man of Macedonia, and prayed him, saying, Come over into Macedonia, and help us.   And after he had seen the vision, immediately we endeavoured to go into Macedonia, assuredly gathering that the Lord had called us for to preach the gospel unto them.*

In one occasion of seeking God's direction as to which place they were to go so as to preach the gospel, Paul and his companion were praying, then suddenly there was a vision, and in this vision, Paul was able to hear a man asking them to go help them at Macedonia. This was a human spirit talking to Paul in a vision!   The human spirit was alive and was on the other side of the sea.   This is just a rare occasion, and mentioned once in the Bible, although there are also stories such as Daniel talking to the angels, king Saul talking to Samuel through a woman (who served as a medium or a mediator between two persons in different dimensions), and John the beloved talking to the elders, angels, and also to Jesus. This is just one of the abilities of human beings, that by God's grace we can communicate to a spirit - human spirits, angels, and God. On the other hand, this ability has also been made known by Satan to his human slaves such as the Satanists, witches, and spiritualists (new age, etc.).

God in his divine providence gave us a unique experience of communication to a human spirit that is in a spiritual realm, by making him to get inside a person's body (like what was done by king Saul to Samuel through the woman's body (1 Samuel 28).

It was God who opened to us this door of experience. Others may not want to believe in this, and others may accuse us of being a cult, but still we are here to testify of the things that God has shown and revealed to us.

Talking to Nanay Elizabeth (a witch that surrendered her life to Christ)

While we were praying, suddenly God moved us to have this experience of talking to Nanay Elizabeth. She entered into one of our members (Krizel/Eagle's Eye), and suddenly we had a conversation. At first, she waged warfare against us, for she still was under the influence of the demon that used to control her as a witch. After we defeated the demon that had control over her, Nanay Elizabeth got back into her own mind, and had a conversation with us, telling us that she was tired and wanted to rest, and that she was looking for peace in all of her, and even asked if God would still forgive her in spite of all the evil things that she had committed. She said that she was a witch, and already has a rank, and got to that rank by sacrificing humans to Satan. She even told us that Satan grants them power, and even promotes them once they committed evil things such as killing people, destroying things, etc. She clearly told us that as a powerful witch, she had the ability to get out of her body (astral projection) and thereby go into the heavenly realm, and from that place begin her evil works as Satan commanded her. As a witch, like in the military, they have their chain of command, and were receiving their own tasks/missions from the king of the devil. The greatest mission that can be entrusted to them is when they will be assigned to attack and destroy a Christian, a pastor, or even an entire church. The mission given to them is dependent on their power and ability to do evil. That night, and even the previous nights, Satan assigned her to attack us since we used to pray night and day, and according to Satan, our prayers hinder his demonic works on earth. Nanay Elizabeth had to watch us for a time, studied each of us, our strengths and weaknesses, and even spiritual abilities, and with the information that she had, made a plan to attack us by the help of the powerful demons from hell. According to her, their work is systematic and is fully organized, for Satan will not tolerate any failure. Often when they failed their mission, they received a punishment from the king of darkness such as a beating, having one part of their physical body destroyed, the killing of one of their loved ones, and the worst is, their own death.

The night she attacked us, the Holy Spirit already gave us a word of prophecy to prepare us for the battle field. Direct communication to God can be a great help, for it can allow us to do an advance strategy and preparations against our enemies. Often unpreparedness and lack of direct communication to God is what makes the church to be defeated by the enemies in the battle field, and this will result in spiritual bondage, trouble, sickness, broken relationships, etc. Remember, the thief comes only to steal, kill, and destroy.

Nanay Elizabeth surrendered to Jesus Christ that night. She was talking to me through Eagle's Eye, and I led her to confess her sins and to believe in Jesus Christ to be her Lord and Savior, and even to denounce Satan over all her life, and that she did. After her repentance of her sins, God forgave her and she experienced the wonderful peace of God that was being sought by her for all of her life. For she came from a family of witches, and all of her life she was raised to became a witch, and even saw some of her relatives die as a witch without the Savior in them, and now they are all in hell. While she was crying and was overwhelmed by the grace of God, we felt the presence of God in the room, and realized God's unfailing love. Hallelujah!

After that night, Nanay Elizabeth still could be in the spiritual world while her human body is in her house (often witches, Satanists, and those who did the astral projection have to hide their body so that their opponents, Satan followers like them, would not see it, for once it was found they will burn it, or chop it up and eat it, and if that happens they will die). By this time, she had her new life in Christ. Her spiritual ability to get out of her body and to communicate to the spirits was still in her, only that now her spirit belongs to God. She told us that God told her that her life will not last; that she will die soon. So, she made us a request of looking after her two sons, and like her, that we should help them get out of the dark and come to the light of Jesus, and to that we agreed.

One human spirit came, one after another. Some were influential, some were just common men, but in the spirit, they are known by the power they possess. We met people like a dean in a university (often atheist professors are Satanists, but not all), businessmen, politicians, military men, religious people, etc. All of them had one thing in common, they were looking for Jesus. They were likened to a wounded soul that needs a doctor to heal them. Or, like sheep that were gone astray, and now were turning back to their shepherd. Or, like lost children that were looking for their Father, like a person that used to live a miserable life and is now looking for the purpose of life: Jesus.

All of them at first fought us hard in a spiritual battle. Often, we suffered from their attacks just before we took the victory over them. Each and every one of them had their own different power. Some were powerful to throw physical sickness on people, and in this we and the children suffered from their attacks for a time, until we overcame them by the grace of God. Some were good at attacking relationships so as to create confusion that would result in a broken relationship, if not dealt with. Some were masters of mental attacks; they can project and whisper demonic things to a person's mind, that if your mind was unprotected, it could make you be confused, be distracted, be worried, and the worst is, it could make you a lunatic/crazy! No wonder that God in Ephesians 6:17 commanded us to put on the helmet of salvation, and I believe this is to protect our mind from the spirit of confusion, and lying thoughts. We know that in the four gospels, Jesus was being attacked by Satan in his mind a couple of times while he was in his fasting for forty days, and his disciples, like Peter, also suffered in this attack for three-and-a-half years, and fell in this for a time, yet by the grace of God were able to recover. Judas Iscariot was overcome by this spirit that led him to pursue money, and betrayed Jesus.

Our enemies had different kinds of spiritual abilities to be used in war. The highest in the rank often would not engage us that instance. They often would send their minions ahead of them, and would engage just when they saw that it fit the situation. One of the sad things here is that they often sacrificed their minions (human spirits) so as to spare their own lives.

Spiritual warfare can be experienced both in spirit and in the physical. The difference between us, Christians, and the slaves of Satan, is that they can fully receive the pain, and even die for it just when they have lost the battle. We, however, by the grace of God, are always under the care of God so as to lessen the pain, or even the casualty if we are harmed.

Ricardo: Dean of the university

Many (not all) professors are involved in Satanism. Here at Laguna we heard one of the universities has this Satanist professor, and he often recruited his students to be members of that group. I heard that policemen used to raid one of their hideouts, a cave, and close it. Many heard this news; this took place at one university at Los Banos.

After our victory over Satan, and we won Nanay Elizabeth back to Jesus, Satan was furious at us, and even sent his powerful human slaves, one after another, to make us their primary target. One of his slaves was Ricardo. He was a professor, and had a high position, both in the school and as a Satanist. He actually was the leader of their group, which some called a coven. With his trained students, aided by the demons (each and every one of them had a spirit guide which is a demon, and this is to protect them and even to empower them), he and his students used to watch over us night and day (they have their shift work in everything), and again tried to find a way to devour us (1 Peter 5:8). Some evil strategies were applied by them to attack us. They sent the spirit of confusion, envy, jealousy, laziness, physical sickness, etc. For a time, we had been hit by these attacks, yet by the grace of God we managed to overcome them, for we are more than conquerors through him who loves us.

We Christians should always be reminded and be encouraged that the precious blood of Jesus is our powerful defense against satanic powers of all sorts. Revelation 12:11: *And they overcame him by the blood of the Lamb, and by the word of their testimony; and they loved not their lives unto the death.*

The Holy Spirit as a teacher in the battle field

John 14:26: *But the Comforter, which is the Holy Ghost, whom the Father will send in my name, he shall teach you all things, and bring all things to your remembrance, whatsoever I have said unto you.*

Psalms 18:39-40: *For thou hast girded me with strength unto the battle: thou hast subdued under me those that rose up against me. Thou hast also given me the necks of mine enemies; that I might destroy them that hate me.*

Every time the enemies planned a surprise attack against us, the Holy Spirit was there to remind, and even to warn us. He often was there to expose the enemy's hidden agenda against us; not to frighten us, but to make us be prepared. Many, due to lack of direct communication from the Lord, were being destroyed by the enemies. They have no time to listen to the Lord's "still, small voice" so as to follow his specific instructions. But God in his goodness trained us in this way of abiding in him. He teaches us different ways to overcome every battle. Since our enemies use different kinds of strategies, we also had to deal with them having different forms of battle plans from the Lord, and in that, our victory was sure.

In a spiritual battle, Satan can send his entire demonic hosts from hell and even mobilize those that are in the earth so as to gather and fight just one church, or one man! This doesn't depend on the numbers, the outside popularity, and materials and money that the church possesses; rather, it depends on the faith of them. We heard where Jesus said in Matthew 18:20: *For where two or three are gathered together in my name, there am I in the midst of them.* So, with just the two or three of you gathered in Jesus' name, asking the Father to let his will be done in this earth, Satan will be threatened enough to send all his forces, just to stop you from your prayer. Remember that at the time of Paul and his companion,

God was turning the world upside down wherever they went, and this made the other churches take the opportunity to gather their strength without any hindrances from the enemies, since they were being occupied (demons can only be in one place at a time).

Our warfare against Ricardo and his students, and the demons with them, lasted for a week. After we one by one defeated his students, we finally faced him in a battle. Like a battle in a movie or on any occasion, you first have to defeat the minions, just before you face the master. Ricardo was powerful, and he even was being aided by the high-ranking demons from hell, even by Beelzebub and Abaddon (occasionally). They tried their best to defeat us, even trying to possess some of our weak members to divert our focus, but we were determined to capture Ricardo. Since God trained us in different kinds of deliverance strategies, we managed to form two groups. One group would have to deliver the possessed members, while we (prophetess and some other members) pursued Ricardo. In the spirit realm the battle arena is wide; it's not limited. Demons use different kinds of tactics to deceive us, even by trying to change their faces, voices, size, etc. It's almost the same as what you see on an animated cartoon movie (we know that the writers of these cartoon movies were inspired by demons so as to clearly portray such detailed ideas of spiritual warfare). After nights and days of warfare, finally we defeated Ricardo and even destroyed all of his demonic weapons and power in Jesus' name (Isaiah 54:17). By the assistance of the angels, we delivered Ricardo from all of the demonic influences in his mind, heart, and emotions (his body was in his room), and thereby made him to surrender his life to Jesus by preaching the gospel. It's true that unless you first cast the demons out from the person, they can't really accept Jesus as their Lord and Savior, even if they want to, since their mind (and heart) is blinded or is under the control of the enemy (2 Corinthians 4:4). He accepted the Lord Jesus as his God and Savior that night, and thereby experienced the wonderful peace of God. He cried joyfully upon receiving God's forgiveness. It was as if he was like a bird that used to be in cage that was being set free for the first time! Even those of us in the room realized God's wonderful presence. The experience, the feeling is vivid. Some of our members, those that have their spiritual eyes and ears open, were able to see the scene completely. They saw the Lord Jesus in a form of light, embracing Ricardo, who was falling down at his feet, while angels were surrounding him, and some demons were in chains and were commanded by Jesus to be thrown into the lake of fire. He was being clothed with a white robe, and was given an assigned angel to guard him until the appointed time of God for him to get out of this world shall come. His students went back to their place defeatedly, yet were angrily planning to retaliate against us. Upon knowing that their leader was captured and was now a child of God, they immediately consulted Satan on who should take over his position. In this, the assistant should take over the position of the defeated leader. There are times in which some lower member, that had an ambition to get the position of a leader, will ask for a duel against the proposed member to take over the leadership, and this will be accepted. They have to fight, and whoever wins the fight shall be the leader, and often this fight ends up in the physical death of one of them! Truly, motivated by greed and arrogance, Satan's slaves are willing to die, and even to kill, so as to be promoted into a high position. A high position means additional demonic power and wealth. The position of Ricardo was being won over by the more evil, crafty, and powerful member. Once he was declared a leader, the first assignment that was given to him by Satan was to kill Ricardo, their traitorous former leader. We know that Satan will not tolerate betrayal in his ranks, and Ricardo knows this. God also told him that he will not live long, therefore he must be wise enough to use his remaining weeks or months so as to prepare his family (for they are also members of Satanism), to serve God.

Ricardo now, as a servant of God

Becoming a new creation in Christ, Ricardo was now having an earnest desire to worship Jesus, and even to serve him.   In

Satanism the highest form of worship service that they can give to Satan is when they offer human blood, or human sacrifices to him. Sometimes this human sacrifice is their captured member that betrayed them; some are those that failed in their mission, and so on. They did these sacrifices to warn others that Satan will not tolerate any failure. There is always a punishment for every mistake; that is Satan's way of rulership. He often sows fear in his slaves, demons and humans alike. Ricardo declared some of their secrets to us, and even tried to talk to some of his students and friends that were Satanists to stop following Satan and begin to serve Jesus, as he was now doing. Some were persuaded by him by the grace of God, but some attacked him and even tried to kill him (both in the spirit and in the physical). For they know that Satan will give a reward of power to those that can kill him. Nevertheless, Ricardo wasn't shaken by this threat from them, but was determined enough to preach Christ to them. Now that he had been set free from Satan's power, he thought of nothing but to help others know this love of Christ that was being shared to him.

The time of Ricardo's departure from this world came. His body was found by the Satanists, and then it was chopped into pieces and was eaten by the Satanists and some witches, again, to set an example to those that will betray Satan. They took his body, but God took his spirit to heaven. Praise God for his amazing grace!

Human spirits in a group of thousands

Spiritual revival took place in the spirit in a massive portion. Before, we used to handle one spirit at a time, then a group of ten, twenty, and fifty human spirits, and now it was being widened by the Lord to thousands of them in a group. At first, we began in a battle, and after they were defeated by us, then they would surrender their lives to Jesus. At this time, God allowed us to face the powerful witches, Satanists, occultists, wizards (male witches) that belonged to a famous, wealthy and powerful family in the world. They tried to dodge us at first, since they were only permitted to engage us once Satan gave them the command. Some got afraid of us; some were interested for greed of power.

Our engagement in warfare toward a powerful group of Satan's slaves happened when they were in a battle against each other. Since Satan's desire is to drag as many souls as he can to hell, he is using humans to do this, and even killing his slaves afterward. Truly, he only comes to steal, kill and destroy, and his slaves are blind, or powerless to get out of this lifestyle, since their only choice to escape from Satan is Jesus. God revealed to us that they were scheduling a battle to the death by the slaves of Satan, and we needed to stop it, for it would only result in the death of all of them. They were promised much more power by Satan once they won this battle. The fight was between the leader and their members against the group. They would use all of their might to win the fight, and they would have to kill their opponents in a way that no one should escape. All this, without knowing that it is Satan's way to kill them all in order to bring them to hell, and find other human slaves. That is how cruel and crafty Satan is.

Lists of battles to the death among Satan's slaves around the world

Russia vs. Germany: This was supposed to happen on July 29, 2015, but didn't because of the sudden death of Brunhilda (the leader of Germany's group). Just before the time of war between these Satanists happened, she arrogantly attacked us, and tried to destroy us, trying to impress Satan. She even was being warned by some of her former co-witches to not seriously engage us in the battle, for it would cost her life, yet she still insisted on her way. In a night of warfare, she challenged a brave princess (spiritual name of one of our members), and even tried to kill her, yet she was killed in return. God will not let his faithful people die in a battle field; that is a sure promise. She was destroyed totally, and even her fortresses. Now her soul is being tormented in hell as a reward of Satan for her foolish loyalty. One of our members saw her in hell. She is in chains, and is being bitten by wild beasts (demons) until nothing is left of her soul, and then she again returns to her complete body, then she again is devoured by the wild beasts until nothing is left of her. The torment happens continually as Satan commanded it. In hell, Satan is a king.

Another battle scheduled was the battle between the group of Satan's slaves from Belgium against the group from Yugoslavia, and this took place on July 28, 2015. Australia against Mississippi took place on July 31, 2015. All of these happened in the evening.

The evening of July 26, 2015, there was a scheduled battle to the death by the group called Peninsula, with its king demon, whose name is Venski. This group has 3,500 members in all. While their opponent was from Yugoslavia, with their demon king named Jolen, this group has 5,000 members in all. Just when the battle began, the human leader was facing the other group's leader and chatting. This is to tell the group to surrender; at least they will give them a little mercy so as to not kill them all. Yet, under the influence of arrogance and pride, none of them has a mind to surrender. They were like a group of people that was hypnotized by their king demon. On the outward, the battle seemed like a real fight, but God allowed us to hear the conversation of the two king demons. They conversed with their own minds (distance is not an issue in the spirit). The conversation went on like this:

Venski: Hey, Jolen! We have been commanded to annihilate them all! So, let us watch them killing one another until no one is left!

Jolen: That is true, Venski! Ha, ha! (demonic laugh)…let us make sure that all of them shall die in this fight, and afterwards king Satan will reward us with more power, and after that we will again form another group!

Both groups came up into the battle line facing one another with their leader in front. Then suddenly God led us to stand in the gap, and catch them all by surprise. It's like in a movie when a cop would appear on the scene and catch all the criminals. When we (often it was prophetess and I, and sometimes the other members who had their eyes and ears open to do this, since I couldn't do it alone, because the Lord hasn't yet opened both my eyes and ears to see everything in the spiritual realm) stood in the midst of them, I immediately declared, "Cease, and stand by where you are, in the name of Jesus!" Without fail, they all became as I commanded them in Jesus' name. Even their king demons would freeze in the name of Jesus (Philippians 2:9-11)! Hallelujah!

All of them were surprised at our unexpected appearance on the battle scene, although many of them already knew us in the spiritual world (demons used to warn their slaves not to engage in battle with powerful saints like us, for it would mean defeat to them, and salvation to their slaves). While they were all standing still, they could still manage to communicate with us through their minds. So, the human leader got angry with us, and even tried to ask us why we were there. We told them all the things that they should know; the plan of their demon king to kill them all so as to bring their souls into hell as Satan commanded them. In that, demons couldn't lie, since in Jesus' name, they were forced to tell the truth. We also told them that we were there to save them from this plan of killing them all by Satan, that we wanted them to get free from Satan. At first, they resisted us, and even tried to curse us, telling us to get away from them, for what was happening was none of our business. Since they were under the satanic influence, we had to first deliver them from that power before we could make them to believe in us; that is in the gospel. Since they were there believing that they were powerful, I went forward and even challenged their leader to test their satanic power against the power of Jesus. Sometimes prophetess did this. Their leader went forward, and I said to them, "Now, try to use all of your might and power against me, and see whether your power can really subdue the power of Jesus in me! But give me your word, that if you will see that your power can't subdue mine, and has no effect on us, then you have to surrender to Jesus by will!" In this they agreed, since they were there because of power, and for the sake of power. To warriors of darkness like them, nothing can persuade them to either fight or surrender, but power.

Their leader moved forward so as to use all his power against me, yet just before he could do that the Holy Spirit struck him with the holy electricity (one of God's powers) all over his body, enough that he really shook violently. This took about a minute (for who can endure God's power?), then suddenly he shouted, "I surrender! I surrender!" This scene was seen by all of their group's members, and even their king demon that was standing still watching the whole event. Then the defeated leader persuaded his members to surrender themselves to Jesus, since he was persuaded that Jesus is much more powerful than all, and that they saw what God had done to him. When they agreed to surrender, I preached to them the gospel and even made them to confess their sins, and ask God for forgiveness, and after they did this, tears flowed down on their faces as they received God's forgiveness. Now, they were not just being apprehended by God's power, but mostly by his love. After we made them to surrender their lives to Jesus, we now faced the two demon kings, and bound them, and commanded them to go back to hell in the name of Jesus, and this happened in an instant. We saw them as if there was a force behind them that took hold of them and threw them in hell powerfully!

These events took place one after another. God revealed to us the schedule and we waited for it, even if it meant that we were to be awake the whole night (since we have differences in physical time all over the world). Our hearts and minds were both captured by the desire to save the souls of Satan's slaves.

Encounter with the Nephilims

Genesis 6:4: *There were giants* (NASB uses the term "Nephilim") *in the earth in those days; and also after that, when the sons of*

God came in unto the daughters of men, and they bare children to them, the same became mighty men which were of old, men of renown.

Nephilims are the children of both angels that took a human form (Genesis 6:1-4) and their human wives. These group of angelic beings rebelled against God as mentioned in detail by the prophet Enoch in his letter. After these angels committed such sin, God immediately condemned them all, and threw them into the deepest part of hell: the pit of darkness (2 Peter 2:4, Jude verse 6). But their children (Nephilims) used to fill the earth, and thereby created great violence, enough that God had to destroy them all through the flood, and only Noah and his family were left. Yet, we all know that the entire race of Nephilims weren't killed by the flood (for some of them were mermaids, and later on I found out that they have a wide place to live under the earth! No wonder that they that are under the earth are commanded to kneel down and confess that Jesus is Lord (Philippians 2:10-11)) and so they continued to exist even after the time of Joshua (the Anakites (Numbers 13)), king David (remember, Goliath belongs to the race of Nephilims; him being a giant was not a result of physical abnormality as some skeptics falsely say, since he had a brother like him (2 Samuel 21:19)), and also at the time of the New Testament, and even now. We heard and even saw some physical evidences of them, their bones and skeletons being portrayed in a museum, and media, although some government agency tried to hide them. I also heard and even watched an interview with a U.S. marine that encountered a red-haired giant in one of the caves in Afghanistan. This giant was fifteen feet in height, had a spear, and armor, and a shield, and moved very fast so that he managed to kill some of the soldiers with his spear. Yet, he was killed by them when they fired at his face. His dead body was being carried by a plane, brought into the camp, and all of them were commanded to not tell anyone the knowledge of the encounter of this giant. However, some of them couldn't help themselves but to share it with others, even to the family members of the soldiers that were killed by this giant.

Nephilims are like us, creation with a spirit and human body, yet their difference is that they have an abnormal body form. For some of them are giants, some are half human, half animal (the lower body was human, yet the upper part up to the head was animal, and others have a human head, yet an animal body, and some are aliens, etc.). Some looked like an animal in their form, so that you may think they are a beast. I saw one video of a living mermaid that was being uploaded on Facebook. The creature was still breathing, and she looked like a huge red fish, yet she had six human breasts, and two arms that were bound by a rope at that time. The video was deleted immediately, for we know that there are groups of people that hide these things. We also managed to see some mermaids here at Laguna (only a back part). They often swim having their tails up, and also many authentic videos of them were shown by people that encountered them.

Like us, they have spirits, and like us, they sinned against God, and like us, they need to be saved by the hearing of the gospel. Yes, you heard me right; they also must be saved by the hearing of the gospel. Since they also can communicate in between the physical and the spiritual world, and also can do the astral projection, like the Satanists, witches, and occultists that we encounter in the spiritual realm, we met them, or should I say, God, allowed us to meet them. There were two groups of Nephilims, regardless of their differences in their physical forms. One of the groups belongs to Satan; one belongs to God. Using the ability that God gave to us, we managed to communicate with them, and even had different encounters within the spiritual world. There were Nephilims under the water, there were Nephilims under the earth, and also there were some of them in the mountains, even caves. Like our encounters with others, we first had warfare, then, after them being defeated by us in the name of Jesus; they decided to fully surrender their lives to Jesus. Truly, once a person is freed from the power of Satan, they can then without hesitation believe in the gospel; for who would refuse to be saved?   It's only the demonic influence of Satan that blinded them to not believe in the gospel, yet after that influence was removed, they began to see the light of God in the gospel, and thereby believed it, and that made them to be saved.

God revealed to us that in the last days, they will again show themselves so as to dwell with people like they did before. Also, that some of them will show themselves powerful enough to deceive even the very elect, performing signs and wonders, portraying themselves to be the false Christs and the false prophets (Matthew 24:5, 23-26, 36).

Seeing and hearing spirits with our physical eyes and ears

One of the abilities that God opened and developed in us is the ability to see and hear spirits with our physical eyes and ears. It seemed like our spiritual senses were combined with our physical senses. Yet this happens only as the Lord permits it, for we are still in the process of spiritual discipline. For what do you think would happen if God would allow you to see the spiritual world at all times, or anytime you want to see it? There would be an imbalance that would take place if this was not managed correctly. God only allowed us to see and even taste a part of it for the sake of convincing our minds. For often skeptics only listen to their minds, to the point of making them spiritually blind. For our faith must be based only on the word of God, and we ought to believe if the word tells us something, even if our mind doesn't understand it.

My encounter in this was somehow different from others, and I know that this was just the beginning. It happened while I was teaching our leaders in the church, and I was in front of them, and we were in the room. My eyes saw a demon in a form of a shadow running on the left side of the church's corner, and then immediately it was gone. I saw it with my physical eyes open, and the scene took place on the terrace of our rental house (the door that separates the terrace was closed at that time). Another instance was while we were in prayer warfare, that one of our leaders was being attacked on his head, and he felt the pain literally. I applied the blood of Jesus for healing, and then suddenly when I looked at the right side of the temple, I saw a human spirit in a form of a shadow. I saw that it had a flat top haircut, and it was walking away from us. I believe this one was the attacker that caused the headache of our member. This experience of seeing through went on deeper, and it came to the point of seeing different faces on the wall, on the ground, etc. One of our sisters from America had the same experience of seeing these faces, and was even able to take a picture of it. This happened after she got baptized by the Holy Spirit and fire. I heard that another person received an experience of seeing through, in that he saw the stories in the Bible happening like a movie before him while reading them.

Prophetess

After my mother got saved, God immediately opened her spirit to the spiritual realm for a purpose. Most of the revelation from this book was given through her. God opened her eyes and ears spiritually, deeper than the other members. God has his own reasons in doing that. One reason is for warfare, one for inquiry, one for character, and some, for a calling. Whatsoever the reason is, it sure will be for the glory of God, and for the salvation of his people. Even Jesus' disciples had their own level of experiencing the spiritual realm with their spiritual eyes and ears open. Most of the time in prayer, prophetess sees the spiritual realm vividly. She saw demons, angels, and the power and the weapons we use every time we wage war. She even was able to see Jesus with us, sometimes in a form of light, sometimes in his human form with his long brown hair, calm loving face, wearing a white robe, and according to her, he is about seven feet in his height. She also was even able to converse with Jesus, and with angels, demons, and also the saints.

Meeting Moses in the garden

One afternoon, while praying, God allowed her (prophetess) to meet Moses in the garden (of Eden). At first, she didn't recognize him, for when he introduced himself, he pronounced his name 'Mosae' (Mosa in Filipino). She was puzzled who this man was, yet this man talked to her and even discussed something that had to do with God's plan, even to our church and family. It was when she asked me who he was, that the Lord told me the Hebrew pronunciation of the name Moses is Mosae, and then immediately I told her that it was Moses that she met in that garden.

While I was doing the record of this event of meeting Moses in the garden, this made me be in awe of God's wonder. We know Moses only in the Bible, yet to speak to him, even if wasn't me who was doing the conversation, I sensed the truth of this spiritual meeting with him in my spirit at that time, and we were thankful to God.

Warrior of God

This spiritual name was given to our eldest brother Rufino. God also opened his eyes and ears in a different level. In a time of our prayer, God allowed him to see the spiritual realm and our enemies, even the angels that assist us. In particular, God is using him to study the end times (some portions). Through his awakened spiritual senses, he asked God for the knowledge of the end times prophecy. God blessed him with the gift of dreams, visions, prophecy, and even interpretations. There also was a unique experience that God was doing through him in the middle of prayer. That was the time when the Lord was making us to go through a different level of the holy fire rooms in heaven. This unique experience was that he was praying while his body was turned upside down! Yes, upside down. During prayer, when he was filled with the power of God, his body was sweating, and he was at the side of the wall, then began to pray upside down. Later, God allowed us to understand the meaning of this experience that we called body prophetic gesture.

Different kinds of high-ranking demons and their functions

Since angels were perfectly created by God, all of them have their own identity and personality, even those that rebelled against him. God in his mercy allowed us to know the high-ranking demons of Satan and their functions. We know that Satan is able to perform all of his demonic activities on earth by dispatching the demons under his command. In war it is imperative for us to know our enemies' identity, power, and weakness so as to make a winning strategy. Failure to know our enemy is what would make us be defeated, often times. Others are afraid to know about demons by believing it will give the demons glory, but I tell you Satan loves to hide himself so that he may able to attack his victim without fail (1 Peter 5:8).

Abaddon: Apollyon in Greek, "the destroyer", (Revelation9:11)

This powerful demon is in charge mostly of attacking Christians in terms of war, and also is often sent by Satan to devastate a place, a group of people, a family, and every relationship. He is filled with anger and dark power, so that often other demons are afraid of him.

Nathan: One of the second-in-command, like Abaddon

Though this one isn't mentioned in the Bible, nevertheless he has significant functions in Satan's kingdom. Almost like the work of Abaddon, he is to execute some important task or evil plan of Satan so as to destroy people, even churches.

Razum: Like Nathan, he also is second-in-command in Satan's kingdom.

This one is the spirit of the fallen angel that was assigned by Satan to guard one of the huge and powerful satanic groups named "Illuminati". In the book of Daniel, Gabriel and Michael fought the fallen angel that was called a "prince of Persia, and Greece" just when Gabriel was to enter into Babylon so as to deliver God's message. In this passage God is giving us the idea that each and every territory on earth has a demon spirit to guard it.

Rank 1: Rahnne: Spirit of falsification; counterfeit

This one is in charge of twisting the spiritual gifts and power. He is targeting gifted and anointed servants so as deceive, and to corrupt them by giving them false messages. Assisted by the lesser demons below, this one can silently get inside of the church by deceiving powerful leaders and ministers. Once it gets inside of a person's body or church, he will immediately twist the message at the pulpit so as to mislead the church away from the true message of Christ, and he also is the one that is empowering the occult people that pretend to be servants of God (fake healers, psychics, witch doctors, etc.).

Rank 2: Dragger: Spirit of greed

One of the Christian writers that also writes about spiritual warfare saw this demon in a form of a man that was having an attaché case, and a wrist watch that he often looks at, although in some visions that the Lord showed to us, this one has many horns, and has a large pointy tooth outside of its mouth, like a hog. The function of this demon is to entice people, even Christian leaders, to become greedy for everything in this world. He is manipulating them to live just to get what they want, without contentment, and that they want to get it no matter what it takes. Assisted sometimes by the spirit of self-centeredness, lying, arrogance, and pride, their agenda is to deceive people by believing that they can only have their rest when they can get what they want.

Rank 3: Beelzebub/Beelzebul/Denlyn: Provoking spirit; prince of dung/flies

In the Bible, this one was mentioned by the religious leaders so as to blaspheme the Holy Spirit that is working in Jesus (Matthew12:22-32), yet without knowing it, they were the ones that were being used by this demon! One of the evil works of this demon is to kill your passion for God, to make you religious, yet you deny the power of godliness. This spirit likely possesses much more demonic wisdom than the rest of them, that according to the Lord, he will rise up in the last days to be the spirit that will stand as the antichrist in this world (Revelation 11:7).

Rank 4: Dudja: Spirit of bitterness, jealousy, judgmental mind, criticism, religion, self- righteousness, and self-centeredness

If other powerful demons focus on attacking the mentality and physical body of their victims, this one has its work only on the emotions of its victim. Since humans are composed of spirit/heart, mind, emotions, and body, this one makes its dwelling in the emotions of those that are enslaved by him. We can observe that there are people that have a problem with their emotions; often we call them emotional. Christian counselors often first diagnose the case of their patients before they give counsel to them, for every case is different from each other.

Rank 5: Lucerna, lying spirit

Satan is the father of lies, and this one is his son that teaches people, both believers and unbelievers, to lie. Lying is telling something that is against the truth (word of God). People often misunderstand lying to be not telling something that people want to know, but I tell you that you can hide a secret from a person and not tell it to them, even if they force you, and that is not lying; it is just simply that you are keeping that secret! Lying in God's word is stating anything that is against the truth. Ananias and Sapphira lied against the Holy Spirit when they said things that were contrary to God's word. They kept back part of the money that came from a lot that sold, and the money was supposed to be given to the apostles (Acts 5:1-11), and they failed to repent of it even after Peter gave them a chance to tell the truth. Because of their sin, God killed them! That is why it is a huge sin to lie against God.

Rank 6: Eleizer: Spirit of confusion

Confusion can be working in our mind and emotions. This demon specifically targets the minds of its victims. Since our mind is often controlling our life, Satan wants to make a stronghold in it. Even the apostles, Paul and Peter, knew this evil work of the enemy against our mind, so that they wrote about renewing our mind (Romans 12:2), and to have the mind that is ready to receive suffering for Christ (1 Peter 4:1). Once the enemy manages to take over our minds, it is difficult for us to have a consistent walk with the Lord, since we need to fix both our heart and mind in Christ Jesus (Colossians 3:1-2).

Rank 7: Rampgei: Spirit of anger

Anger can be as disastrous as fire (Proverbs 27:4). As human beings we have emotions, and one of them is anger. It is not a sin to get angry, but what we say or do when we are angry often makes us to sin. That's why Paul says in Ephesians 4:26-27: *Be ye angry and sin not...neither give place to the devil* (in your emotions!). I heard a minister that testified that one of his weaknesses is his emotions - that he often turns wild when he gets angry. All of us may be experiencing the same struggling with our emotions, yet the Bible tells us to have self-control, which is one of the fruits of the Spirit. Remember that it is easier to destroy rather than to fix things around us. So, don't let your anger ruin what God is building through you.

Rank 8: Ruhner: Spirit of stubbornness

The first king of Israel, Saul by name, fell victim to the hand of this demon (1 Samuel 15:23), and even the nation of Israel with its leaders and priests were often guilty of being a stiff-necked/ stubborn people. This demon is manipulating people in their hearts and minds so as to resist God's word, so as to continue in their lives of sin until they die. This is also one of the reasons why the first generation of Israel fell dead in the wilderness after forty years of wanderings, and weren't able to get into the promised land, while Joshua and Caleb did. For us to escape from the demonic influence of this demon, we are to follow God's instructions that say: *To day if ye will hear his voice, harden not your hearts, as in the provocation, in the day of temptation in the wilderness* (Hebrews 3:7-8).

To listen to God means salvation, and to go on to stubbornness means destruction.

Rank 9: Nazer: Spirit of shame, self-condemnation and cowardice

"Low self-esteem" is what we always say about a person that lacks courage. Psychologists have their own explanation of this kind of spiritual problem of us humans. Yet if only we will see, even us believers, that God gave us the spirit of love, power, and self-control, and not timidity/fear (2 Timothy 1:7). There are many reasons why a person would fall victim to this kind of spirit, yet by the help of God, and by the love and care that we can patiently give them, the victim can possibly get out from this demonic manipulation so as to experience spiritual freedom. Often its victims falsely believe that they have already lost their value as humans, and to make it worse, they end up going to suicide. The power of the gospel is to heal the broken-hearted (Luke 4:18), and it takes forgiveness when a person has bitter feelings inside his/her heart, or at least, the stronghold of this spirit has to do with unforgiveness. We encountered people totally oppressed by demons, having bitterness in their hearts, as the stronghold of the enemy in them. Sometimes healing for the people that are victimized by Nazer was a long process, for it deals with both mind and emotions. The deeper the wound is, the harder and longer the process of healing will be, yet it is worth it. That is why it takes patience and love on behalf of the relatives of the victim for them to be able to help the person be freed from the bondage of this spirit.

Rank 10: Dalhie: Spirit of confusing emotions, depression, and diverting spirit

Almost the same with the work of Nazer, and Eliezer, Dalhie focuses on attacking the emotions of its victims. When the Holy Spirit left king Saul, he was troubled by this demon (1 Samuel 16:14-15) of confusing emotions. He wasn't attacked physically, but only in his emotions. That's why he often turned outrageous when he showed his anger towards David, and even his son Jonathan almost got killed by him (1 Samuel 19:9-10, 20:30-33). In my personal experience, I saw how this demon terrorized a person who is a believer and a leader of the church. This man had a grudge in his heart toward his wife, and it happened when they had an argument that this man turned outrageous towards his wife, even before us! It was as if he became a different person at that time, that he didn't care for anything except just to release his anger, yet after the shameful event, his shameful feelings went deeper into his spirit, so that he almost wanted to disappear from us. This person was a leader in the church for so many years, yet was a victim of this spirit of confusing emotions. People like them can be compared to a child that loves to build his place to play, yet when he gets angry, he destroys all of it without hesitation, only to feel sorry after he destroys it. Some of our church members, and even leaders, had a personal encounter of this demon themselves for a long time. It is by the grace of God that they managed to overcome this demon so as to resist it, and it went out of them.

Rank 11: Dunger: Spirit of imitation

Dunger's work often supported Rahnie's - counterfeiting the gifts and power of the Holy Spirit in the believer's life. The spirit of imitation is busy trying to imitate the work of God in order to mislead many. Satan can make himself to be an angel of light (2 Corinthians 11:14) in order to deceive the church; yet by the gift of discernment we can test him in a way that he will be exposed. Often this spirit works in the life of the false prophets/ministers, mimicking the ministry of prophecy, healing, signs and wonders, and miracles. They also can imitate a person's movements, face, voice, and body if necessary. In our experience with this spirit, while we are praying, it will speak to us using one of our member's voices, so as to interrupt us. I experienced it myself many times. Its work begins as a little degree, then goes to a higher degree of deception, enough to make a person believe that he is serving God, yet he is not. This spirit is the one that made the sons of Sceva to imitate the ministry of Paul at Ephesus (Acts 19:13-17), yet when this group encountered it, it was a group of much more powerful demons in a man possessed. They paid the price of being beaten naked and were cast out themselves! We need to always test the spirit of a person by evaluating his message, and his fruit (character, motive) so as to avoid being victimized by this demon.

Rank 12: Dungel: Spirit of corruption

Corruption has to do with bribery, dishonesty, etc. A pastor that preaches the gospel so as win money (not souls) is a victim of this spirit; also Israel's judges and leaders were often working under the demonic influence of this demon. It made them to declare a sinner to be righteous, and a righteous man to be guilty of sin. Even Pharisees used to have this spirit so as to condemn the innocent and to praise the guilty, and when a righteous person begins to twist the justice of God's word for the reason of personal gain, that is a result of them being under the control of this demon. One of the false prophets in the Old Testament, Balaam, likely fell victim to this demon. He used to prophesy so as to receive gifts from kings, yet when he was to pronounce a curse against Israel, he was rebuked by God, who used his donkey to speak, thereby correcting his madness (Numbers 22:28-35)! Even the believers that turned, becoming servants of Satan, false prophets that were mentioned by Peter, spoke lies so as to have material gain from their victims (2 Peter 2:13-14).

Rank 13: Dezziel: Spirit of monogram, apparition, lust and denial

An image of Jesus on a tree, on a wall, an image of Mary and some saints that were worshipped by people - these are just the work of this demon of spirit of apparition. The Roman Catholic Church and their members fall victim to this spirit. Since this church followed the wrong teachings about idol (images and sculpture) worship, this spirit freely moves in them and deceives them in way that they can't get out of that delusion. Here in the Philippines, men used to follow such kind of foolish worship of this apparition from demons. Even Moses warned the Israelites of this sin of worshipping graven images of the created things (Exodus 20:3-5). This demon also can put a demonic illusion into our minds, so as to lure us by falling into lust. How many times we experience this kind of temptation from this demon while we are in the middle of prayer, or while we are seriously meditating on the word of God! His work is to create a different image of God so as to make you turn away from him, and follow that deception. This demon also can work by the help of the spirit of imitation and of counterfeit, so as to deceive a Christian who has their spiritual eyes and ears open. This demon can give you false visions and dreams so that if you are not aware, it will make you fall into error. Some of the members that went out of our church had fallen victim to this demon. I remember when Andrew used to attend our prayer meetings passionately with his family. Yet it happened when I didn't see him and his family attending our gathering, it made me feel uneasy; something wrong was happening. Andrew went on not attending our gathering until he decided to get out of our church, without telling me the reason why. I tried to ask him the reason why he and his family stopped attending the church, yet he didn't say to me one word. Hannah is his cousin that invited him to the church, and she was one of our leaders before. She told me that the reason why Andrew stopped attending our fellowship is because of the vision that he saw the night that he was praying with us. In that vision, he saw me (Pastor Joven) standing before him, wearing a black coat with a red tie, like the appearance of Dracula. This demon made me appear to him like a Dracula! And Andrew immediately received and believed that vision without testing the spirit! How pitiful he was. After years of not attending with us, I learned that he and his wife are separated, and he still was deluded in his mind. See, Satan will do everything to make you be destroyed, by making you to get out or stop following a spiritual leader, so that no one can protect you from him.

Rank 14: Darren/Jezebel: Controlling spirit, dominant spirit, worry and fear

In the Old Testament, one of the double-minded kings, Ahab, had this spirit due to his connection to his witch wife, Jezebel (1 Kings 21:1-16). Jezebel made Ahab fall under her demonic spell by putting this spirit on him. Led by this demon, and by the evil advice of his wife, king Ahab stole Naboth's vineyard, and because of this, both he and Jezebel were killed by God. Darren attacks the prophets of God, and often is busy working with the counterfeit gift of prophecy, also known as false prophecy. Thyatira church was guilty of entertaining this spirit within them, to the point of allowing it to mislead God's servant by the way of false teachings and false prophecy. The Lord says that this woman (the person that is possessed by Darren) made God's servants sin against him by teaching them to commit fornication and to eat food (false teachings and prophecy) sacrificed to idols (Revelation 2:20). God's judgment on her is the same as it was for Ahab and Jezebel from the Old Testament; sickness that leads to death if they will not repent. Those that operate in the ministry of prophecy and teaching must be aware and be careful of this spirit of Darren, and must be humble when they are confronted of being guilty of doing the evil works of this demon, enough to repent so as to be forgiven. Failure to repent after a confrontation would mean a much deeper spiritual bondage by this demon.

Rank 15: Rommer: Spirit of arrogance

If pride is the crown and armor, arrogance is the sword or weapon of the sinner against themselves! It's true that after a great victory, men and women of God fall into sin because of pride and arrogance. Physical achievement can blind us so as to makes us not see the pit of destruction before us. Apostle Paul, after experiencing so many victories in his mission, and being able to go into heaven through a divine revelation (2 Corinthians 12:1-4), was allowed by God to be punished by Satan through the thorn in the flesh that he had. He even asked God three times to remove it, yet God's answer seemed to open the eyes of the apostle so he could see the danger laid by the spirit of pride and arrogance before him. God sees that the hearts of his servants seem weak when they are in their physical glory, so that they can easily fall into the temptation of pride and arrogance. He has to protect them by removing that physical glory from them, and often it hurts. Many pastors nowadays are eaten up by pride and arrogance, so that their hearts and minds are captured by Satan, so as to make them feel superior to others, even God! Yes! Pride and arrogance can make you think that you are wiser and more powerful than God! Look at Satan; he was in heaven, and was favored by God among the angels. Yet when he deceived himself by thinking that he, too, can be on God's throne so as to be worshiped by the angels, he fell into hell. It is not the will of God for his servants to fall away from his grace.   That's why he, in his mercy, will do any necessary corrections, training us so as to protect us from falling. We only have to humbly accept those corrections for us not to fall into the place of the accuser of the brethren!

Rank 16: Drezzdje: Unforgiving spirit

The Bible say unless you forgive those who sinned against you, your Father in heaven will never forgive you of your sins. Likewise, Satan knows this, so he lures people by making them have a grudge in their spirit against their enemies, instead of forgiving them as the Lord commanded. Unforgiveness can be a stronghold that invites demons to stay inside a person's body and life, making them live miserably. Yet the grace and mercy of God are abundant towards those that will obey God by forgiving their opponents, and releasing a blessing to them, instead of asking for vengeance. It is written that the Lord says: *Vengeance is mine! I will repay, saith the Lord* (Romans 12:19). In one of our experiences with deliverance, a woman who had this spirit was being tortured by different spirits that made her a lunatic, or crazy. We tried to deliver her from demons, and managed to only cast out some, yet other demons stubbornly remained inside of her body. I was disappointed upon seeing that our efforts in setting her free from demons seemed to fail, yet the Lord in his mercy spoke to us, "Unless she forgives all the people that hurt her, she can never get out from under those demons." Then we found out that she had a grudge toward people, especially toward her husband who abandoned her. We tried to talk to her and tell her that she had to forgive them if she wanted to totally be free from demons; she refused, and this made us to leave her, and give her time until she decides to release all the anger and grudges in her heart against those people. You see, unless we get rid of all sins, demons can still find their way into us so as to steal, kill, and destroy our life.

An encounter against the spirit of imitation

1 John 4:1: *Beloved, believe not every spirit, but try the spirits whether they are of God: because many false prophets are gone out into the world.*

We experienced a different attack from this spirit, both in the spirit and in the physical. In one instance this spirit tried to imitate the voice of one of our members in order to confuse us, or even to frighten us. One afternoon, I was tested by this spirit. My sister went out in the morning, and then while we were praying at about 6:00 p.m., I heard the voice of my sister downstairs. I thought that she had come home, since I heard her voice loud and clear. Then after the prayer, I went down to check on her, and to my surprise she still hadn't yet come. Then the Lord told me that it was the spirit of imitation that was imitating her voice, and that we must be careful not to immediately believe everything, but to always test the spirits. This also can happen in the spirit through a vision, dream, or seeing through. Its work is to imitate so as to deceive. Once an imitation is carelessly accepted, it will become a deception, and once the deception stays for long, it will become a corruption.

On different occasions, we got engaged with these different high-ranking demons, even Satan's second-in-command. Truly it's hard to face these powerful demons in a fight. Sometimes the battle took place all night until the next day. As humans we were exhausted, but the grace of God allowed us to overcome each and every fight in time. Most of the time the warfare happens when the demons get inside the physical body of one of our members. After doing that, they will use the body of that person so as to create trouble by loud shouting (often to attract attention from the outsiders), destroying things around, and even hurting people, and also to stop us from praying. In that we have to get engaged in a deliverance work by casting out the demons from that person's body. Deliverance ministry can be hard and difficult, and it can often fail if the person will not participate in the deliverance ministry. For example, if the spirit that gets inside of the person is the spirit of Drezzdje/unforgiveness, we can't immediately cast it out unless the person forgives all the people that offended her or him. If the person won't forgive, we can't make that spirit get out of her body, since it has a stronghold in her life. That stronghold is an unconfessed sin of a person that serves as a legal ground for the demon to stay in that person's body. That's why it is very important that the person that is undergoing deliverance believes Jesus, so as to submit himself. That will result in the demons being resisted.

Sometimes, deliverance can be very difficult and could cause physical damage when the person possessed by demons is acting playful, and listening to the lying words of Satan, rather than to the word of God. In this case, deliverance ministers should be cautious and patient enough to handle a long-range battle. If the resistance of the demons is strong, it is simply because the person has united his will to them, and in that case the minister should first talk heartily to the person, so as to persuade him to believe in God. If the person doesn't agree to the process of deliverance, it will not be successful and will just be a waste of time. In this case, the deliverance minister should be patient enough to wait for a person until she surrenders her will to Jesus so as to repent of her sins and forgive her offenders, and if that happens, demons will lose their foothold in the person's life, and we can cast them out without resistance from them.

Demonic attack through the unbelievers

2 Timothy 2:24-26: *And the servant of the Lord must not strive; but be gentle unto all men, apt to teach, patient, in meekness instructing those that oppose themselves; if God peradventure will give them repentance to the acknowledging of the truth; and that they may recover themselves out of the snare of the devil, who are taken captive by him at his will.*

Satan can use his demons, human slaves, and the unbelievers (those outsiders that have no connection with occultism) to attack us, the Christians. Sometimes our faith can be truly purified just when we are being tested by way of the unbelievers, for often they will attack us physically. Our experience with this happens in different ways. In one instance, they threw a stone at the roof of our house church, and in one instance they directly threw it inside our house. Praise God that no one got hurt by this; only a few things were destroyed. This caused irritation, anger, worries and fear in us. Nevertheless, God assured us that he will protect us, even the children. From throwing stones, it would have escalated up to almost direct physical fighting, if God had not intervened. We also are attacked by them verbally. People on the outside often stare at us demonically. They often call us crazy people, a cult, and weird. That is how the world really treats us who are living in the spirit. To them, it's just a normal thing if you are a drunkard, gambler, addict, gossiper, etc., but when you give yourself to prayer, Bible study, and worship, they consider you an enemy, since they are threatened by the righteousness of God in us, and are convicted of their sins.

The most affected (and for a time, carried away) by this physical attack were the women and immature men in the church. They were provoked by this kind of assault against us. The children also were being maligned and insulted in their school, but we managed to teach them to be wise in dealing with that kind of false accusation. I observed that as we go through this kind of persecution, both the adults and the children became stronger than before. Truly the testing of our faith shall be for our own good.

We read in the Bible how Jesus' disciples were provoked by this kind of demonic attack from the unbelievers. John and James got angry when they were rejected at Samaria, and even asked Jesus to allow them to kill those people by commanding fire to come down from heaven (Luke 9:51-56) like Elijah did in the Old Testament times. Even Peter struck the ear of a man that went up against them in the garden to arrest Jesus. Our character must be tested by different forms of persecutions, until we are like Jesus. Unless that happens, our enemy will always find ways to destroy us, our ministries, and our families.

Physical attack by demons and human spirits

Demons and human spirits, although they are in the spirit form, yet they can still attack us and even hurt us physically. The worst result of this attack, if they are not conquered by us, can be physical death (untimely). We in the church are being attacked physically by the enemies that were in a spirit form - human spirits aided by powerful demons. These attacks can be physical illness, laziness, dizziness, losing things (by stealing), and physical death through a nightmare (cardiac arrest while sleeping), car/plane/ship accident, etc.

Pastor Joven stabbed at the heart by a wizard in the form of a human spirit

2 Corinthians 4:8-10: *We are troubled on every side, yet not distressed; we are perplexed, but not in despair; Persecuted, but not forsaken; cast down, but not destroyed; Always bearing about in the body the dying of the Lord Jesus, that the life also of Jesus might be made manifest in our body.*

Satan most of the time will attack us the moment we are not prepared. Often this was effective against us; complacency and negligence are the biggest reasons why we often fell into Satan's snare. At the time when some members got out of the church to go back to the world (some of them were my brothers and niece), this made me depressed, and this gave an opening to Satan's slave to strike me. One wizard (male witch) named Raul, from Malinta, Los Banos, was commanded by Satan to watch me until he could find an opportunity to kill me. That afternoon, I was filled with grief and sorrow for the soldiers that ran away from their battle field, and this wizard struck me with a wooden peg in my chest, straight to my heart (this happened in the spirit, not physically). I was at the window, when I felt the sudden pain in my chest, and my upper body got numb. My wife was there, and upon hearing me agonizing because of the pain, she at first thought that I was just joking. I told her that I felt pain in my upper body, and that she was to call prophetess (my mom) and pray about what was happening. The pain was real; it was as if something was being struck into my chest, yet in the physical realm I couldn't see anything. When my wife went to the prophetess and shared what had happened, immediately God showed her in a vision what had taken place. She went up, for she was on the first floor of our rental house at Sucol, Calamba, washing the clothes. Then the Lord instructed her to massage my back so that the blood would run normally, then she applied healing in the name of Jesus. I got relief. After that she went into the room and fought back against Raul in the spirit. In that, she made him ran away from the battle scene.

This was just one of the many instances of satanic physical attack against us by the enemies. This attack was followed by the children who fell from the roof down to the ground; some stumbled on the floor with their foreheads hitting the floor, and some got sick for almost one month!

Satan also tried to cause car accidents against us, only this was stopped by us in prayer. Every time our enemies were planning to harm us, God on the other hand, revealed it to us so we could be prepared. You may say, how about the angels, were they not there to guard us? Yes, they were. They are always there to guard us, and to protect us from the enemy. Yet, we also must be reminded that we are God's soldiers, and that he wanted us to learn to fight at all times. Sadly, there were many of our people that fell into this kind of satanic attack. There were those that got killed in a car accident, plane crash, ship that sank, heart attack, etc. These things that kill people untimely are not the will of God. It was Satan's evil work of stealing, killing, and destroying us humans. People tend to blame God when tragedy happens. They would ask and say, "Where was God when that car accident happened? If he is powerful and all-knowing, why did he allow that to happen, even sometimes to his children?" God really is all-powerful and all-knowing, and he is present everywhere. He was there just before Satan would plan a tragedy, and also there when it happened. He is there beforehand to warn people about a tragedy, yet people are too busy to listen to that warning. He is there even just a minute, or a split second before something happens, trying to persuade people to call upon him, yet they are too intellectual and too rich to call upon him (look at the Laodicean church in Revelation 3:17). How many tragedies were planned by Satan, and were revealed by God to his people, and his people fought back to stop Satan, and they won over those tragedies, yet people around were too busy to know this!

Disasters: an instrument of punishment

Isaiah 45:7: *I form the light, and create darkness: I make peace, and create evil: I the LORD do all these things.*

Amos 4:7, 11: *And also I have withholden the rain from you, when there were yet three months to the harvest: and I caused it to rain upon one city, and caused it not to rain upon another city: one piece was rained upon, and the piece whereupon it rained not withered. I have overthrown some of you, as God overthrew Sodom and Gomorrah, and ye were as a firebrand plucked out of the burning: yet have ye not returned unto me, saith the LORD.*

Disasters like super typhoons, earthquakes, volcanic eruptions, tsunamis, plagues, famines, and war are just instruments of physical punishment given by God to mankind because of their evil works. How many of these were supposed to take place, yet were stopped, and some were delayed, because God led us to pray that these things would not happen? However, in the places in which Christians were sleeping, their places were visited by these disasters, and were destroyed. People were killed; houses fell down, and so on. God doesn't want anybody to die perishing in hell, but that all might be saved in the name of Jesus. But due to stubbornness and unbelief, many died untimely. In God's righteousness he will not allow any sin to go unpunished; that's why he provided a sin offering for all: the blood of Jesus on a cross. Yet, even after the sacrificial lamb has been offered up, still many choose to reject the gospel. Mercy triumphs over judgment, therefore before God would send disasters to every country, region, and even family or individual, he first would send them a warning. Often this warning is brought in by his messengers, the prophets. God went down to Abraham first before he sent his angels to Lot in order to rescue him from the upcoming fire and sulfur that was to destroy Sodom and Gomorrah. His appearance to Abraham had to do with the fulfillment of his promise and to reveal to him the plan of destroying the two evil cities, and that was for the purpose of intercession. Abraham asked God to withdraw his punishment for the sake of the righteous, yet God still sent the fire and sulfur, since there was not such an exact number (ten, Genesis 18:32-33) of righteous people that lived in that place. We all know that Abraham was just thinking about Lot and his family when he asked God to save the righteous (Genesis 19:29), yet if only we will listen to God's desire of saving the world, which is that even the unrighteous might be forgiven, we will begin to pray the prayer of Jesus on the cross, saying, "Father, forgive them, for they do not know what they are doing!"

On the other hand, when God also was about to send his punishment to Nineveh, he first sent Jonah so as to preach the message to them, without looking for any righteous men. Jonah was at first hesitant because of his personal grudge against the Ninevites, for they were enemies. Nevertheless, the message was preached, and the people listened and repented - from their king, to the babies, and animals. God in his mercy withdrew the punishment. If only we people of God would often intercede to God to withdraw the punishment, and not just for the sake of the righteous, but for the sake of his righteousness, surely God can again send people like Jonah today to a people that are living like those in Sodom and Gomorrah, to save them, and not to punish them.

Visions of heaven

Houses in heaven

John 14:1-3: *Let not your heart be troubled: ye believe in God, believe also in me. In my Father's house are many mansions: if it were not so, I would have told you. I go to prepare a place for you. And if I go and prepare a place for you, I will come again, and receive you unto myself; that where I am, there ye may be also.*

To have our house in heaven is just one of the many glorious promises that God gave to each of his children. Many misunderstand the truth of this promise. Every promise has a condition to be met; therefore, for us to have this promise, we must comply to its condition: faith. Many mistakenly believe that all Christians will have a mansion or a house in heaven, but I tell you, a house in heaven is again one of the rewards for our righteous work here on earth, and its size and structure depend on our diligent work here on earth.

One of the visions that God gave us is the scene of our own house in heaven. We also found out that God put our house in a compound that was named after the fellowship or a local church we are in. To us, our houses are in the 'Christ the Living Word' compound. On a gate of this compound you will see the name of our church wonderfully fixed there. It has different designs, and was clothed with gold. When we entered into the compound, the first two houses that we could see in front are the houses of both the pastor and his wife. The next is the house of the leaders. We also observed that each has their own unique design, and the design and the color are dependent upon the character and what is the favorite of its owner. We also saw angels were busy constructing each and every house. They are using materials such as gold, diamonds, and different kinds of precious stones. The materials of our house can only be provided every time we are doing the will of God here on earth. We all know that God designated to each of us our specific work or ministry in the church, and every time we faithfully fulfil that ministry, every second, minute, and hour, strength, effort, and money that we spent so as to fulfill that ministry would equate to adding up materials to be given for the construction of our houses. Having this knowledge, we also understood that each and every house is different in its size and glory, depending on the passionate work of each person in the church while on earth. We saw that there were houses that looked like a Bible; there were some that looked like a musical instrument (harp, piano, guitar, etc.). There were some that looked like a sword, some looked like an eagle, some looked like a plane, some looked like a ship. All of them are glorious in their appearance, although they are different in their sizes and designs. We also learned that each house's foundation could have a one-foot diamond to be built in it every time a person saves a soul on earth by the gospel. Evangelism is the main task God gave to the entire church on earth, and this can be done by all in a different way, according to the task entrusted to each one. One may evangelize a person by means of prayer, one by the means of inviting a person to the church or to the Bible study, one maybe by giving a Bible tract, and one maybe through giving food and clothing. There are so many ways to bring each and every soul to Christ. When the angel would report each soul that was saved on earth, it was being listed in detail: the time, the place, the person that preached, the one that invited him/her, the one that prayed for that person, and mostly the specific message that struck the heart of that person. God would make sure that shall be listed in detail, and they shall be receiving their due reward. No wonder that the Bible tells us to not be weary in doing good, for we will reap a harvest if we do not give up (Galatians 6:9). Your good works on earth, done by faith in Jesus with the motive of love and humility, can mean materials to be added to your house so as to make it huge in its size and height. In heaven, there is no limit in anything. I heard one testimony about the great houses of the famous evangelists like John Wesley, Dwight L. Moody, and more. They all, because of their passionate work in preaching the gospel, now have a great and glorious mansion in heaven. Some had a four hundred story building mansion, some reached up to a thousand, and even tens of thousands of story mansions in heaven. I learned also that each and every room, or story, of this mansion is comparable to the size of a football field here on earth! Yes, it's unimaginable. Paul once said, "No eye has seen, no ear has heard, no mind can conceive what God has prepared for his beloved!" The glory of heaven hasn't yet been comprehended by any human mind. It's unfathomable! That's why Satan was angry when he was cast out from that place when he sinned, yet when we humans sin against God, he made a way for us, and that is Jesus.

Flowers and places in heaven

Isaiah 66:10-14: *Rejoice ye with Jerusalem, and be glad with her, all ye that love her: rejoice for joy with her, all ye that mourn for her: That ye may suck, and be satisfied with the breasts of her consolations; that ye may milk out, and be delighted with the abundance of her glory. For thus saith the LORD, Behold, I will extend peace to her like a river, and the glory of the Gentiles like a flowing stream: then shall ye suck, ye shall be borne upon her sides, and be dandled upon her knees. As one whom his mother comforted, so will I comfort you; and ye shall be comforted in Jerusalem. And when ye see this, your heart shall rejoice, and your bones shall flourish like an herb: and the hand of the LORD shall be known toward his servants, and his indignation toward his enemies.*

There are different flowers in heaven. They are all beautiful and sweet in their color and fragrance. Amazingly, they are all alive, and we heard them singing praises to God. Every flower given to each individual to be planted in their garden is determined by the personalities of each person. There are flowers that can be seen on earth, and there are flowers that can only be found in heaven. All in heaven are full of beauty and life.

There are also different places in heaven. In the Bible we can only read about places like the throne room, in which God the Father is at the center, and the four living creatures before the throne, and twenty-four elders sitting on their own thrones surrounding God, worshipping him there (Revelation 4). In heaven there are different beautiful, glorious, wonderful places. I perceive that we have to spend the whole of eternity so as to visit each and every place in heaven in detail. There are huge and vast libraries that contain innumerable books. There are also conference rooms in which important issues can be discussed by Jesus with the saints and the high-ranking angels. Some issues have to do with the events that are happening here on earth, and the plan of God to save mankind. Everything has a proper place in heaven. Every person that God is using now to do his great commission here on earth has his guardian angel there attending the conference. The detail of each and every person's service so as to fulfill their mission is openly discussed in that place; the length of time, people to work with, places, material provisions, and even the sufferings that they are to go through, until they have finished their mission on earth. There are also places or rooms of different kinds of God's power, gifts and provision. There are rooms of holy fire, holy electricity, poisonous thorns, wisdom, knowledge, prophecy, descendants, tongues, prayer, etc. Surely God has a designated place for everything in heaven. Everything there is in order, and is in the unity of the Spirit. Rooms also for provisions are designed and diverse depending on each person's faith. To a person that is full of faith, great missions and provision can be entrusted, and to each and every trial that a person overcomes, more is added to his mission and provision (Matthew 25:14-30).

There are also places for relatives to meet in heaven. I found out that not all saints that are in heaven can have their home close to the throne of the Father, for that place is reserved for those who can lay down their lives here on earth, carry their cross, and follow Jesus. Those people received a better place in heaven. This shows God's faithfulness in his word when he says that he will grant each one according to their own works. Those saints that repented of their sins and were saved at the last hour of their life have their own place in the farthest part of heaven from the throne, and very rarely can they see Jesus there. All their lives, they lived away from God, and still by God's grace at the last moment of their lives, God still had to forgive them when they repented of their sins. Now in that place they are grateful to God for his amazing grace, that he still forgave them, and brought them into that place to spend eternity, not in hell, which they deserved. Many in that farthest place of heaven from God's throne are people that were famous, rich, powerful, and almost were being worshipped by men while they were here on earth, and they almost received such vain worship of men. Now they understand who is due of the true worship and the service of men.

The crowns

2 Timothy 4:8: *Henceforth there is laid up for me a crown of righteousness, which the Lord, the righteous judge, shall give me at that day: and not to me only, but unto all them also that love his appearing.*

Isaiah 62:3: *Thou shalt also be a crown of glory in the hand of the LORD, and a royal diadem in the hand of thy God.*

Crowns are also promised to be given to those that overcome satanic temptation here on earth. Knowing different crowns here on earth, with their different sizes and glory, gives us the understanding that this also is true in heaven. Crowns in heaven are different in their sizes and glory, and this depends on the good works of their recipients. Every crown in heaven varies according to the precious stones set into it. All are made up of gold, and like the principle of building the mansions in heaven, the crowns in their glory are the same. There were precious stones to be set in each crown, and every time the owner of that crown is faithful to God, more stones are added to his crown, and its design becomes more glorious. In the Bible there were lists of different kind of crowns, like the crown of life (James 1:12, Revelation 2:10), golden crown (Revelation 14:14), crown of glory (1 Peter 5:4), crown of righteousness (2 Timothy 4:8), and crown of rejoicing (1 Thessalonians 2:19). The Bible doesn't say these are all the crowns, because the Lord also mentioned to us the crown of a warrior, crown of a prophet, a teacher, pastor, an evangelist, an apostle, an intercessor, a mediator, etc. I observed that crowns may vary by the person's faith and ministry. That is why when Jesus warns us to not allow others to steal our crown (Revelation 3:11), this crown has to do with the crown of service/ministry. For once a person becomes negligent in his spiritual service, his crown will soon be given to others in God's appointed time (Matthew 25:28-29).

Armory in heaven

Ephesians 6:10-17: *Finally, my brethren, be strong in the Lord, and in the power of his might. Put on the whole armour of God that ye may be able to stand against the wiles of the devil. For we wrestle not against flesh and blood, but against principalities, against powers, against the rulers of the darkness of this world, against spiritual wickedness in high places. Wherefore take unto you the whole armour of God, that ye may be able to withstand in the evil day, and having done all, to stand. Stand therefore, having your loins girt about with truth, and having on the breastplate of righteousness; And your feet shod with the preparation of the gospel of peace; Above all, taking the shield of faith, wherewith ye shall be able to quench all the fiery darts of the wicked. And take the helmet of salvation, and the sword of the Spirit, which is the word of God:*

In heaven there is a place which is called the armory of heaven. This is the place where all of the armory to be given on earth to every saint to use in the battle field can be found. In this place, there are various rooms of armories. In one room we saw armor like breastplates; this armor is to protect the upper body of the bearer. It varies depending on the bearer's spiritual position/calling in Christ. There is a breastplate for the generals, captains, lieutenants, down to the lowest position of each soldier in God's camp. There is also the belt of truth, the shield of faith, shoes, and helmet of salvation, and some that are not listed in the Bible like the sword of faith, arrow of hope, and bow of wisdom. It seems that all of God's word represents a weapon and an armor to be given to God's people. In that armory, there is also a room that contains materials to be used for spiritual communication, healing, etc. Truly God has provided all of our needs according to his riches and glory in Christ Jesus.

Visions of hell

Proverbs 7:27: *Her house is the way to hell, going down to the chambers of death.*

Luke 16:22-23: *And it came to pass, that the beggar died, and was carried by the angels into Abraham's bosom: the rich man also died, and was buried; And in hell he lift up his eyes, being in torments, and seeth Abraham afar off, and Lazarus in his bosom.*

Every time we gather to pray, God allows each member that has his spiritual eyes and ears open to see different visions, even visions of hell.

In some visions, God showed us our relatives that have already died and now are in hell, even our biological father. My mother saw him being tortured by a group of demons. He was carried by them, and forced to go inside of a large pot, and after that some demons took a fish hook and struck his neck, then pulled it out without mercy! My father cried and even shouted louder because of the horrible pain that he felt. After that, one demon took a jar of boiling oil, then poured it on my father, who was still inside the pot. This made his body to melt down like ice cream when it was exposed to heat. My mom couldn't help herself but to feel pity toward my father because of the suffering that he experienced in hell. Since demons were aware of our presence in hell, they tortured our father twice as much as usual as a form of retaliation against us, and this will be throughout eternity! Not just our father is there, some of our other relatives are also there. Our grandfather, two uncles, aunt, and even my childhood friend is there. They are experiencing a different torture in that place and it is also dependent on their evil works that they did while they were still alive. My grandfather was being pierced by a spear in the lower part of his body since he used to be a womanizer. My uncle used to be a drug addict and a gambler, so in hell demons forced him to drink a gallon of acid that made his body to swell inside, and even to blow it up due to the strong chemicals that entered him. One couldn't really imagine the pain of torment in hell. Even by just trying to listen to their cries and loud shouting, we can't really understand it, unless we are the one that receives that torment. My mom also saw her cousin in hell. Surprisingly, not one of us knew that she had already died, for she lived in a faraway land of Catbalogan, Samar, while we are here at Luzon. My mom also hadn't yet met her, not even once. In hell, this woman was in the middle of a pit of fire. Then suddenly demons pulled her out to torture her in a different way. She was naked, and little by little demons tortured her by slicing her body, beginning from her breasts and downward. While this woman was in pain, she happened to look at the place where my mom was, and said to her, "Hey, Yolanda, (my mom's name) I'm your cousin, Imelda! Why are you here? Please get out of here, or at least try to help me get out of here!" My mom at first was confused, for she hadn't met her, although in her heart she knew that this woman was a relative of hers. This woman told her that she had died, and she even asked my mom to tell her household to do everything so as to not go into the place in which she was now. When we finished our prayer meeting and we had our sharing time, my mom shared this, and we were amazed. I immediately tried to contact our relatives from Samar so as to confirm this thing, and I found out that it was true. She died by a heart attack. She lived apart from Jesus, and died apart from him, and now she is in the place apart from God's presence, for hell is the place of no God, only torment forever and ever.

Ricardo, my childhood friend

One of the people that also were seen by church members was Ricardo, my childhood friend. I had heard the news of his death; he was stabbed by a knife in his chest by one of his enemies, on a night that he was drunk. He even managed to run to his home, and when he reached the door, he fell down on the floor dead. He was just twenty-four at the time that he died, and his friends cried for his untimely death. He was seen in hell, running, afraid of demons, while demons were giggling in pursuit of him. Since demons are stronger and faster than a soul in hell (the weakest demon can be a thousand times stronger and faster than a human soul in hell), he was caught by them and was put in a big jar. Then suddenly, he was pierced by different spears, and he cried out loud in a way that would almost blow out our ear drums if this was the physical world. After he was pierced, he also was brought into a place where there is boiling oil, like a huge cauldron. He was put in the middle of it, like a chicken soaked in boiling oil by a cook. His full body became a fried human in that kind of torment. He tried to beg demons to stop the torture, but the more he asked, the more demons would become excited to torture him. It seems that demons delight themselves in torturing souls in hell. It gives them pleasure every time they hear and see a human soul being tortured in hell. This young man was being described to me by our church member, and the description fit Ricardo. I pitied him. But I couldn't do anything as to help him out of that place. It's too late for him; it's too late for them that are now in hell. While people are in this world being busy with their physical lives, souls in hell are there being tortured by demons in a different manner, without rest, night and day.

Hell has different places of torment. Every soul that ends up in hell will be in a place that is assigned by Satan to them. With the place and the demons, the soul will be punished horribly. We also found out that, for now, those that were experiencing the most painful torment in hell are the people that once served God, yet turned their backs on him for different reasons. They are there, and their torment was being specialized by the king of hell, since they used to torment Satan and his demons while they were in the service of God, and now as an act of retaliation, they have prepared a special torment for them in hell. Those that once were pastors, elders, deacons, musicians, and even theologians were receiving the worst punishment in hell. One former pastor of a big church ended up going there in hell because of the sin of greed, and stealing money from the church so as to be used for his carnal life style. This pastor once had a mega church that used to have at least five thousand attendees in their gatherings. He first served God whole-heartedly, and endured sufferings and different kinds of trials, yet when God blessed him and his church with money and materials, he began to focus his life on earthly things, and even preached the same to his congregations. Years went by, and he began to live life carnally, and began to commit evil things behind the pulpit. He even had women that asked him for many things, that made him to steal the money from the church in order to be given to them. Even after committing these evil deeds, the Holy Spirit was convicting him of his sins, and pleading with him to repent. Yet he was that stubborn and evil enough to resist the Holy Spirit and continue the life of sin. His lamp died out, and he spiritually died again. One day while he was driving his expensive car, he had an accident that took his life, and then he was dragged by demons there to hell. Satan prepared a different special torment for people like him that ended up in hell. There is a torment that this pastor was being put into a coffin, and he was surrounded by demons, then after that he was pierced with spears by demons without mercy. Inside his coffin his pitiful soul was being crushed by the spears, and this made him to be in terrible pain that couldn't be lessened by just crying or shouting. His crying and shouting because of the pain made the demons torture him, for it made them happy. After this torture, he was carried away by demons into another place of torment. By this time, he was put onto a conveyor, and he was greatly afraid as to where that conveyor would take him. When he reached the end of the conveyor, we saw that it was an instrument that was used to crush animal meat into pieces. When he went through that instrument he was crushed into pieces, like meat in a can. Demons were jumping while laughing upon seeing what had happened, and the pastor's body turned to be made whole again, while the demons were there, waiting for him until he became complete again so that they could bring him into another place of torment. This really is too terrible! Yet, the demons said, there are still different torments that awaited that pastor that are much more painful and horrible, and this made the pastor to shake in his body violently because of fear. There were many of them in that place experiencing a different torment night and day without rest, and there are still many that are coming from the earth, because of sin. While the churches are very busy trying to feed their sinful desires, this place awaits them. For the few who have decided to live in the spirit, heaven is their portion.

Conference room in hell

Isaiah 5:14: *Therefore hell hath enlarged her, and opened her mouth without measure: and their glory, and their multitude, and their pomp, and he that rejoiceth, shall descend into it.*

Matthew 16:18: *And I say also unto thee, That thou art Peter, and upon this rock I will build my church; and the gates of hell shall not prevail against it.*

Hell has many rooms, and it enlarges itself. Every time a soul goes down to hell (in a minute, we saw multitudes going there!) it enlarges itself, and this means more work for Satan to steal more, to kill more, and to destroy more! Hell has its place called a conference room. In this wide and huge room, Satan and his high-ranking demons discuss their evil plans to be executed on earth. Their purpose only focuses on one thing: to kill souls and drag them to hell. Since the church is the body of Christ empowered by the Holy Spirit to destroy their demonic works, Satan focuses their major plans in destroying the church, and their plan is to divide the church. Satan knows that a kingdom that is divided against itself will not last, so it would be a great achievement for them if they can make the body of Christ wage war against one another. He also knows that spiritual unity of the church would attract God's anointing, and that would soon result in a spiritual maturity of the church (Psalm 133, Ephesians 4:11-14), and if this would happen, his dominion on the earth will come to an end.

Demonic attacks against the church

The church is not who she is in the physical, but who she is in the Spirit (often it is in a perfect contrast). Satan knows that the power of the church is in the Spirit, and once it would join to the Holy Spirit, it would become unstoppable, and it would begin to destroy his stronghold on the earth. So, his job is to keep the church from coming into the presence of God. That will make her to become weak, little by little. I will list some of Satan's plans against the church and how he executes them.

Making them to become ignorant of the word of God

Hosea 4:6: *My people are destroyed for lack of knowledge: because thou hast rejected knowledge, I will also reject thee, that thou shalt be no priest to me: seeing thou hast forgotten the law of thy God, I will also forget thy children.*

Since the word of God is the foundation of our salvation (Matthew 7:24-25), Satan and his demons are doing a hard task to remove the church from her foundation, to make her defenseless and powerless. As prophetess and I were listening to one of the meetings held by Satan with his high-ranking demons in hell, their conversation went on like this:

Satan: Okay, I want that accursed church that was built by that man that I killed on a tree to perish in any way possible! If any of you that are in here will help do this, you shall be greatly rewarded by me! Ha, ha, ha (demonical laughter)!

Rahnne/Spirit of falsification: My lord, I will twist the interpretation of the Bible. I will make them believe what is lies, and reject the truth!

Satan: And how can you make it possible?

Rahnne: I will send people, sealed by sin, to conduct a Bible conference that will teach the leaders a different gospel (2 Corinthians 11:3-5, 14, Galatians 1:6-9). This different gospel will make those leaders follow money, materials, and popularity, and that will make them carnal. They will soon lose their appetite for the Holy Spirit. These church leaders will even make them receive money from my servants, and this different gospel will be called by them, "a new light", and many shall follow them in this delusion! Ha, ha, ha!

Satan: Magnificent! Do it and I will grant you the power to succeed! Remember also that I will not tolerate any failures!

Dragger: My lord! I will entice the church leaders to pursue all the world can give them - luxurious cars, planes, gadgets etc., mansions, beautiful clothing, honor, and power, and will trick them even to worship you, just to have as much as they want! This will destroy them! I will seduce the pastors and the leaders to get involved in business, and will try to hypnotize them with the material benefits that they and their family could have once they grab it. Rahnne will throw them those passages, verses in the Bible, that would seem to agree with this by twisting their minds. Once they get in this trap, their spiritual appetite will soon die down, and they will begin to listen to their minds, and even will make the Bible to follow their minds!

Satan: Brilliant ideas! Do it, and you will succeed!

Beelzebub: My lord, I may add a much better idea than the two of them! I will even make many of the pastors and the leaders to prioritize their tradition rather than their conviction, as I did from the time of that man that you killed on a tree! I will make them listen more to men's point of view, instead of the Bible. These leaders will begin to compromise their faith from a man-made idea of leadership that focuses on popularity! I will make them seek man's favor and respect; I will even make them force their people to follow them, and threaten those that will not with the message of condemnation. In this, I need Lucerna, Jezebel, and Rommer, since this is a huge task.

Satan: Finally, Beelzebub! You came up with crafty thoughts! That's why I like you the most! Ha, ha, ha. Go, and Lucerna, Jezebel, and Rommer shall follow you!

Following this, Rahnne and Dragger both got angry with Beelzebub, and even threatened him.   We observed that even though demons are united in destroying Christians, they still have no love for each other, and are in a constant war and envy toward one another. The father of lies keeps on lying to them, even from the beginning when they followed him in their rebellion to God, even up until now. All of them were being cruelly ruled by Satan.

Eleizer: My lord, your servant shall be very busy with the backsliding Christians, for them not to be able to repent until they will die in that state, and we will drag them down all the way here in hell! Once they are here, they will be yours to destroy! I only need Ruhner/Spirit of anger, Nazer/Spirit of shame and self-condemnation, and Drezzdje/Spirit of unforgiveness to support me in this huge work.

Ruhner, Nazer, Drezzdje: What?!! You want us to submit to you? You (foul-mouth words), we will kill you first before it will happen!

Satan: Hey, hey! You three, shut your (foul words) mouths! You are as foolish as the sleeping Christians on the earth when they would rather sleep than pray, and watch TV than read their Bibles! Don't you know that I put that magnificent plan into the beautiful mind of Eleizer? Now, go and follow him!!

And in this, once Satan already made his decision, it will be the final word.

Dungel and Dezziel: My lord, we will work together to attack only the pastors and the leaders of the church! Once we capture the head, the entire body shall follow! We will send beautiful young women into the church, to pretend to be new members, and will soon target to seduce the pastor, and the male leaders. And to the women, we will send young handsome slaves to destroy their faith. We will even make them to pursue cosmetics, jewelry, and good clothing, until they became blinded and deafened by us!

Satan: That is a great idea! Do it and I will give you all you need so as to become successful! Demons to assist you, power, wisdom, and even human slaves! Only make sure that you will not fail, lest you will be greatly tortured here!

Dungel and Dezziel: Yes, my lord!

Satan: The rest of you, continue to do your work, and be diligent! For we need to drag more souls here! I will greatly reward those that will kill more people, especially Christians! And I will greatly punish those that will be coming back because you have been cast out by them! Now, dismissed!!

In this their meeting was adjourned.

***

Aside from the evil things that were being discussed above, Satan still has many plans of destroying the faith of every believer so that they would end up turning their backs on Jesus and following the way of the world again. Once this happens, Satan for a time will use that person to destroy the faith that he/she once embraced in such a way that many would stumble and fall like them. Then they will be killed by him so that they will not come again into repentance and that they will go to hell when they die.

I also will add some evil works of Satan against Christians that would make them become unfruitful in their lives, so as to make them scatterers, and not gatherers of the flocks.

Making them pray less

Matthew 26:41: *Watch and pray, that ye enter not into temptation: the spirit indeed is willing, but the flesh is weak.*

Prayer is our act and time spent with the Lord. Though there are many forms of prayer, still through this we can enter into God's presence daily. I often say, "Prayerless Christian life is a powerless Christian life". Jesus reminded his disciples on the last night that he stayed with them that they should be watchful and pray so that they would not be deceived. Every time we enter into God's presence, our Spirit can absorb all that God made available for us to be absorbed - peace, comfort, power, gentleness, wisdom - and our faith grows in him. This is the reason why Satan doesn't want us, Christians, to pray in a way that we can get into God's place. He is that serious in moving you away from your prayer room/place. Sadly, many are not aware of this and often fall into Satan's snare enough to weaken their prayer life. We know from the Bible that miracles happen every time God's people pray; yet with the condition that they would pray with a humble heart that is turning away from sin and seeking his will (2 Chronicles 7:14).

Another truth in prayer is this: Satan may not be able to remove you from your prayer, yet he will make a way for your prayer to not have an answer. There are many passages in the Bible that promise us of God's answer every time we kneel down and pray, yet it's not just our outward kneeling down, and the lifting of our hands that would assure us of God's answer to our prayer request, rather, it is a heart that is humbled by his grace and is full of faith, believing that what he promised he will be able to make happen.

Bigger prayer, bigger obstacles

Satan hates us when we begin to pray, for he knows when we pray, we began to yield in the Spirit. He also is greatly afraid just when we begin to believe the bigger things of God, and when we begin to ask him to let it be done in our lives on the earth. If he can't make you stop praying, at least he will make you to not receive what you asked for. In the Bible we read stories that tell us how Satan tries to stop Christians from receiving their prayer requests. Daniel began to ask God to fulfill his promise of bringing back the Israelites to Jerusalem as he began to read the letter of prophet Jeremiah (Daniel 9:1-3). He was led by the Spirit to ask God for that, and was determined to receive his answer by fasting. Even when Satan tried to stop him from that prayer by sending his high-ranking demons to stop Gabriel the messenger from bringing the answer to him (Daniel 10:12-21), the angel said it took him twenty-one days in the spiritual world just before he had a breakthrough by the help of Michael, one of the archangels. We also need to remember that during that time, Daniel was in his prayer and fasting for three weeks (21 days, Daniel 10:1-3). We all know that it was king Cyrus who was used by God to fulfill this promise, and this was even prophesied by prophet Isaiah (Isaiah 45:1-5). Daniel's faith was even greatly challenged when Satan tried to stop his prayer life (during this time, he still was praying for the bringing back of the Jews to Jerusalem), by using his friend, who was a king at that time, Darius. Darius was enticed by two of the three presidents that he appointed over his kingdom, who were filled with jealousy toward Daniel, to provide a law that would forbid all his inhabitants to pray to any other god, except to him alone (Daniel 6:4-10). In the New Testament we are told on many occasions to continue praying until we receive an answer (Luke 18:1-8, 1 Thessalonians5:17, James 5:17-18). We understand that this attack against the life of Daniel was just to stop him from praying, but the prophet wouldn't be persuaded, even by the threat of losing everything, even his life. We know that his friend Darius even tried to rescue him, but man's efforts are futile if Satan is on the move - God is the only way out. Daniel determined to pray, even after knowing that he would die from it, by being thrown into the lion's den (Daniel 6:14-24). We know the end of the story. By faith, Daniel shut the mouths of the lions, and so defeated Satan. Bigger prayer, bigger challenges, and the greatest challenge that we can face is the losing of everything, even our life. Yet if we are that determined to deny ourselves just to obey God, we will surely be on the winning side.

Nowadays, the reason why Christians can't ask for the bigger things of God to happen in their lives is the lack of faith, and in lacking of faith, Satan is involved. If he can't make you to stop praying, he will at least make you to stop believing the bigger of things of God. As the Lord Jesus said in Mark 11:22-24: *Have faith in God. For verily I say unto you, That whosoever shall say unto this mountain, Be thou removed, and be thou cast into the sea; and shall not doubt in his heart, but shall believe that those things which he saith shall come to pass; he shall have whatsoever he saith. Therefore I say unto you, what things soever ye desire, when ye pray, believe that ye receive them, and ye shall have them.*

Making them self-centered

2 Timothy 3:2: *For men shall be lovers of their own selves, covetous, boasters, proud, blasphemers, disobedient to parents, unthankful, unholy...*

Self-centeredness destroys everything. If unity is to build up, self-centeredness is to break up! How many Christian relationships are destroyed by people that are motivated by self-centeredness? That's why the first requirement that was told by Jesus to his disciples so as to follow him (preaching the kingdom of God), was to deny themselves. Often, a group can be determined as to whether it will last or will be easy to give up, depending on their motivation. If Jesus is asking us to lay down everything for the sake of his kingdom, Satan is making people to lay down Jesus so as to have everything! No wonder that the requirements of being a disciple are very high: you have to lay down, or leave everything behind - your mother, father, husband, wife, children, siblings, and even yourself! When Satan tried to entice Jesus, he showed him the world's glory and splendor (Matthew 4:8-9). The same evil strategies are being offered by Satan to many Christians, especially to their leaders, even now. While Jesus was asking us to be a servant of all, Satan is enticing us to be served by all. If you are to choose Jesus, you have to forget yourself, but if you are to serve yourself, then you are choosing Satan over Jesus. How many pastors are now in hell being tortured by demons because of the sin of self-centeredness? And still, how many are yet coming into this place of torment that are on the earth at the moment, because of this sin? The sad part is that they are being followed by many in their self-centeredness, while they are going into the place of destruction awaited by the master of lies! Brethren, the call to live by the Spirit so as to not gratify the desires of the flesh is always being whispered by the Holy Spirit in our hearts daily; we only have to listen to him and follow him.

Making them rely on the flesh and not on the power of the Holy Spirit

Galatians 3:3: *Are ye so foolish? Having begun in the Spirit, are ye now made perfect by the flesh?*

Flesh against the Spirit means heaven or hell also. I saw pastors that try to imitate the power of the Spirit by using their flesh. Some of them used to even deceive their congregation so as to idolize them. I know fake healers are doing this, but to hear that a pastor is doing this? This is absurdity! I watched a video of a pastor doing this. One of their members was told that he had been cursed by a witch, that something was being imputed inside his stomach. Then this member was laid flat on the floor of the church, and the pastor went down to him from the pulpit, and put an oil all over his stomach, then pretended to remove something from it. But I observed that while he was doing it, he was holding something by his three fingers, only two fingers were used by him to touch the stomach of that man. Then in the end, he pretended to be taking out mice from his stomach, and the crowd was fooled by this man.

Another truth of this fleshly work in the church is the constant shaking of the people every time they get filled by the power of God. Some used to fall (slain in the spirit). I'm not against this physical shaking, for we, too, used to experience it when God filled us with his power. It's true that our human bodies can't contain the power of God when it flows like a river in the church, and in the Bible there are many things like that, but we have to understand that we ought not to stay from what we feel or have in the physical (shaking, being slain), rather that we have to understand the message in the Spirit. In this book I explain the message of these physical reactions of our body, with some biblical passages, when we got filled by the power of God.

This turning from the Spirit to flesh also happens when the church clings on to man's head knowledge, rather than to the Spirit's wisdom and revelation of the knowledge of His will. Many boast of their denominational pet doctrine, and even the teachings of their favorite theologian, without the proof of God's power (1 Corinthians 4:18-20). While Jesus promised true signs of power of the Holy Spirit for those who believe (Mark16:17-18), many ministers nowadays fail to show this power by just idolizing the man-made teachings of those that used to battle the false teachings of the false Christians during the time of middle ages. I saw how these people came up into extremity in their pursuit of this systematic form of false teaching, that they almost came to the point of spiritual blindness! There are those who forbid people to speak in tongues (if no one would interpret as misinterpretations of 1 Corinthian 14:28); they also do not believe in prophecy (1 Thessalonians 5:20), since, according to them, the Bible is complete so that there is no need for one to have prophecy. They even make a biased statement saying, "There many false prophets today," yet if you will ask them about the true prophets, they couldn't give you even one. It appears that they only are against the spirit of prophecy. You will see them not performing any signs and wonders, miracles, casting out of demons, and things that were performed by God through his people in the Bible, and many are following them! Their understanding of the scriptures is even distorted, and they feel threatened when you come up disagreeing with their beliefs. I happened to meet them many times, trying to persuade them of the imbalances that they teach. Yet, after so many approaches, they still remained stubborn in their dogmas. Mostly these people are unfruitful in their work, and are arrogant and prideful. They have their boast in their dogmas and teachers, rather than in the Lord and his power.

Making them unholy; twisting holiness

2 Timothy 3:2: *For men shall be lovers of their own selves, covetous, boasters, proud, blasphemers, disobedient to parents, unthankful, unholy...*

Isaiah 1:22: *Thy silver is become dross, thy wine mixed with water:*

Even now, churches embrace the systems of the world. They tend to side themselves with the god of this world and become an enemy to God himself. We heard how many churches accepted same-sex marriage, gays and lesbians, and transgenders to be in the church without convicting them of their sin, for to them "we are no longer under condemnation," and God says, "Don't judge!" (yet what God really meant is that we must learn to judge not according to our human mind, but according to the spirit (John 7:24). They are using the scriptures to back up their false claims, making evil good, and good as evil! They formed their own way of holiness - holiness that values man's point of view and not the word of God. For in the word of God is the conviction of sin, that men might understand to live life according to God's will. We know that homosexuality is an abomination to the Lord and that it has no place in the kingdom of God (1 Corinthians 6:9), and in this we are referring to the evil acts of men, not to the men themselves, for God is always calling forth those who live life as homosexuals to come into repentance. They lowered God's standard of holiness so as to please men and approve men's viewpoints, and thereby be friends with them. We know churches allowing worldly dances to be danced in the church, and worldly songs to be sung in the church in worship! They mix the wine (Spirit) with water (world) in their worship service to God, and this makes God to disapprove them. Satan is the mastermind of this abomination. How many pastors out there are like these so as to make the youth fill their church? Some call it a holistic approach of the church to the unbelievers. They just value physical fellowships and the number of attendees, not the fellowship that God requires, which is in the Spirit and in truth.

Making them complacent and negligent

Matthew 26:40-41: *And he cometh unto the disciples, and findeth them asleep, and saith unto Peter, What, could ye not watch with me one hour? Watch and pray, that ye enter not into temptation: the spirit indeed is willing, but the flesh is weak.*

Ephesians 5:14: *Wherefore he saith, Awake thou that sleepest, and arise from the dead, and Christ shall give thee light.*

Any group of soldiers, regardless of their strength, numbers, and weapons - if they are sleeping, they are useless and helpless! The same with Christians that are in the state of spiritual complacency and negligence: they are useless and helpless. Jesus at the passage above was in his great trouble. He was in agony, and his disciples who were supposed to be with him watching and praying were sleeping! And he rebuked them by saying, "Watch and pray!"

Satan is very good at making us sleep until he is able to put us into bondage and get inside of our house and take all the good things he can. This truth can be applied both in the physical and in the spiritual realm. That's why the call to makes ourselves awake and praying is always there daily.   It is when we begin to focus our heart and mind on the things of this world that we will fall into this kind of satanic work. Satan is using the TV, radio, media, and the passions of this world as a snare in which he can catch every serious Christian, since the hypocrites already belong to him. Prayer and serious study of the word of God with the desire to apply it is the key to spiritual awakening, and this must be consistent. How many revival gatherings would only last for weeks, months, and years, simply because there is no consistency from the heart and mind of the leaders, and the major reason why they are inconsistent is that their motive is wrong in asking for revival. Unless one would always spend time with God in word and in prayer, even if you are making yourself busy with what you call ministry, and seem like you are bearing fruit in the physical, still you will find yourself one day sleeping at the time when you are supposed to be awake. Every spiritual warfare (our life of service to the Lord is a warfare) has its own rules, form, strategies, and time to be considered, to assure the victory. Most of the time Christians are ignorant of this truth.

Rules: It must begin in the spirit, and will be extended in the physical (Ephesians 6:12). Most of the time we do it in a reverse mode; we do it in the physical by seeking to increase our money, material possessions, positions, and church members, and this is due to our ignorance, and this assures not our victory, but our slavery to Satan. We can't defeat our enemies that are spirits by who we are, or what we have in the physical! We have to confront them in the spirit.

Form: All war in the world, it maybe civil or world war, is physical in nature/form, in that they use physical weapons and force. But not us Christians. We are being told by the writers of the Bible, anointed by the Holy Spirit, that our warfare is spiritual, so it is up to us to use the power of the Spirit and not of the flesh (Zechariah 4:6, 2 Corinthians 10:4-5). To rely on the power of the Holy Spirit means victory, but to ignore it means a defeat to us. How many of us falsely claim God's promise in the scripture without a proper understanding of the Lord's mind in his word? As a result of this, we fail, and being defeated, we tend to throw on God the blame of our mistake! The Lord doesn't want his people to live in spiritual ignorance and complacency. He wants us to become wise according to his word (Proverbs 1:2-9).

Strategy: (Proverbs 11:14, 20:18) If you can know your enemy, the chance to win the battle is sure. Strategy in war often happens not in the battlefield, but inside the camp! Just before we are to send our people into the battlefield, they are first to be trained of everything that they are supposed to know and have - the skill of fighting, knowledge of weapons, and the plan. I saw Christian leaders ignorantly send their people into the battlefield without proper training, and this is to the harm of them! How many of those people that were being sent into the battle field without proper training were defeated, and are now Satan's prisoners of war, yet they are still in the church doing their respective ministries in the physical! These people are often the reason why the little ones of Jesus in the church get hurt and stumble. If we are to win, we are to know God's plan, and be determined enough to make it happen. In the Bible, every time God's people seek counsel from him, they win, yet every time they ignore his word, they fail! Satan is sneaking behind the church, and would take an opportune time to go beside us so as to pretend to be the Holy Spirit, with the intention of distorting the word of God, yet by the spirit of wisdom in prayer, and by the knowledge from God's word, we can do the same thing that Jesus did to resist Satan by saying (Matthew 4:10): *Then saith Jesus unto him, Get thee hence, Satan: for it is written, Thou shalt worship the Lord thy God, and him only shalt thou serve!* The best strategy that we can apply in the battlefield often comes from our intense prayer and our earnest desire to obey the will of God.

A warning! As of now, there are many that have tried different kinds of man-made systems in the church so as to determine their victory in their ministry. With that man-made system, they back it up with scriptures, and this made them fall into ignorance. We ought not to use the scripture to back up our claim or system; we have to follow the scripture by the wisdom provided by the Holy Spirit and not to make it follow us!

Time: Ecclesiastes 3:1,11: *To every thing there is a season, and a time to every purpose under the heaven: He hath made every thing beautiful in his time: also he hath set the world in their heart, so that no man can find out the work that God maketh from the beginning to the end.*

Time is one of the very important gifts that God gave us. How we use it is our response to him. We are told that we wasted our time before (Ephesians 2:2, 1 Peter 4:3), and now that we are in Christ, we need to redeem the time (Ephesians 5:16) so as to use our present that leads to the future - all for the glory of God. In war it's the same; time can be one of the big factors of winning, and also losing. A wise general should know how to use time in the battlefield. How many offensive attacks were victorious because they were done at the right time, and how many failed because they were done untimely? In war at the Old Testament times, king David had in his army (1 Chronicles 12:32): *And of the children of Issachar, which were men that had understanding of the times, to know what Israel ought to do...* These people seemed likely to be gifted in studying the time so as to use it properly in war, and David recognized God's gift in them. In war there is a time to camp (training), time to march to the battlefield, and a time to wage war, and for us to know which one we are supposed to do first, we need to do an inquiry of the Lord, and even seek people who have the ability, like the children of Issachar, to understand

God's time. We ought not to try to march to the battlefield without a proper training in the camp, and we also need to march in the battlefield just when the Lord gives us the go signal. Failing to comply would make the soldiers have an over stay in their camp, and that would soon become their comfort zone of sleeping. Also, don't try to wage war if what you need is to be trained first. That made many of our comrades get defeated in the battlefield, and they now are still in the enemy's spiritual prison cell; they need our help to set them free. So, don't waste your time; rather, utilize it.

The power of Jesus' name

Philippians 2:10: *That at the name of Jesus every knee should bow, of things in heaven, and things in earth, and things under the earth; And that every tongue should confess that Jesus Christ is Lord, to the glory of God the Father.*

The scripture above is true and powerful! We can cast out demons in the name of Jesus, and deliver a person in that powerful name. That shows the truth of the scripture. In hell, when the Lord brought us there, we waged war with the demons in hell often. They were surprised upon seeing us infiltrating their territory. Hell is filled with gloom, crying of the tormented souls, black smoke, pits, fire, cells, chained demons, and demons in every direction, doing their tasks given to them by Satan. When they saw us, some of them ran away from us to escape out of fear. I found out there were times that it was because of the presence of Jesus, and sometimes the presence of the Holy Spirit. There were times also of us being there that the Lord wouldn't show himself to us, or even to demons, and this made the demons to attack us, trying to catch us to put us into one of their prison cells. But they were surprised when we fought them using the power of the Holy Spirit: holy fire, holy electricity, and holy poisonous thorns, and all kinds of weapons of war that are available to fight them like axes, shields, arrows, and swords. We often were on the winning side when we stood firm and fought them by faith. The most powerful weapon that we can have is the power of Jesus' name. In one of our warfares against them in hell, I commanded all of them to stand firm without doing anything (freeze) in Jesus' name, and without fail they became like a sculpture before us, without even moving a single muscle! Praise God! Disregarding their rank, powerful demons are all powerless in Jesus' name. At one time, we asked them to kneel down, and they knelt down in Jesus' name. If only Christians would really live by faith and execute their power and authority over the demonic hosts of Satan, they would begin to realize that power, and that would make them believe more in the promises of God, and would make them to live a victorious life in the spirit and in this world.

Satan chained in hell

Revelation 20:1-3: *And I saw an angel come down from heaven, having the key of the bottomless pit and a great chain in his hand. And he laid hold on the dragon, that old serpent, which is the Devil, and Satan, and bound him a thousand years, And cast him into the bottomless pit, and shut him up, and set a seal upon him, that he should deceive the nations no more, till the thousand years should be fulfilled: and after that he must be loosed a little season.*

The passages above had already taken place at the time when Jesus died on the cross, and was resurrected the third day. Many of us were ignorant of that truth, and praise God for the revelations. The night when Jesus was with his disciples in the upper room, he clearly stated in John 16:11: *Of judgment, because the prince of this world is judged.* And in John 14:30: *Hereafter I will not talk much with you: for the prince of this world cometh, and hath nothing in me.* Also, in John 12:31: *Now is the judgment of this world: now shall the prince of this world be cast out.*

Satan is both the prince of this world that is judged already, and that came to arrest Jesus through the unbelieving people on the night when Jesus was in the garden of Gethsemane after his prayer, and this is the same Satan that is called the dragon, the old serpent, the devil, that was already bound by an angel right after Jesus was declared victorious over the power of darkness in his resurrection. Paul clearly states in Colossians 2:15: *And having spoiled principalities and powers, he made a show of them openly, triumphing over them in it,* and that happened right after his death on the cross, and was confirmed by his resurrection!

In hell, many times God showed us the place in which Satan's throne can be found, and he was there in a shackle. Often, we saw him in a form of a handsome, masculine, giant angel that had a dark presence. In that figure, we saw his former glory while he was still the servant of God, just before his rebellion (Ezekiel 28:13-17). Of all the angels that were created by God, he was the most beautiful, powerful, and wise, until the day he rebelled against God, and was cast out of heaven and thrown down in hell. Satan can change his image into an enormous ugly serpent, with wings, and a long tail filled with spikes at its back. In this form, he's mostly like a dragon, and in seeing us before him, he got angry toward us, for in that place we beheld the truth of him being defeated on a cross. He was there with his feet in a huge chain. He cursed us with all kinds of demonic curses, and even tried to point his ugly finger with a sharp end at our faces, and even threatened us. But when he did it, and beholding Jesus on our side, he immediately withdrew himself when Jesus just glanced at him. It appears that Satan can easily be provoked, and is still filled with arrogance and pride even after being there in chains. There were times that we went there without Jesus showing himself, and in this Satan felt unrestricted, maligning us, even saying lying words. Of all the statements that he said against us, one captured my attention. He said, "Ha, ha, wait for me, wait for me, just when I am released here from this chain, and I will again rule the world greater than before! And I will persecute you, and will kill all of you, but, if you will bow down and choose to serve me, of course I will spare your life!" Satan really knows the scripture and is trying to distort it, yet he knew then that all of it shall come to pass. He went on saying, "That one that I crucified on a tree! Ha, ha, we will meet again in war, and this time I will be gathering the most powerful army that the world couldn't ever imagine! He defeated me temporarily, but I will take my vengeance, vengeance is mine! And I will destroy all of you on the earth, all of you that rebel against me, and I will torture you and make you to suffer greatly, but again, ha, ha, if you will repent and once again decide to come back to me, and will bow down and serve me, I will show kindness to you, and will forgive you, and once again will clothe you with the richness and glory of the world that the man that I crucified couldn't give you!" Every time Satan spoke, we observed that he couldn't (or forbade himself to) speak the name of Jesus directly. I read one of the testimonies from our brethren that also used to be in hell, that when a demon, or a human slave (in a form of a spirit) would mention the name of Jesus, that Satan upon hearing that powerful name would immediately fall onto the ground from his throne. In this, he threatened his human slaves not to mention that name again, or he would kill them, but when demons would mention that name, he would torture them into pieces, and this is the reason why demons on earth would really do everything so as to not declare that Jesus is Lord. But when they are cast out by a Christian in Jesus' name, they will be thrown back into hell, and they will be dragged before Satan, and Satan would really punish them severely due to their failure, and to set an example for others.

At the time of deliverance

Luke 9:37-42: *And it came to pass, that on the next day, when they were come down from the hill, much people met him. And, behold, a man of the company cried out, saying, Master, I beseech thee, look upon my son: for he is mine only child. And, lo, a spirit taketh him, and he suddenly crieth out; and it teareth him that he foameth again, and bruising him hardly departeth from him. And I besought thy disciples to cast him out; and they could not. And Jesus answering said, O faithless and perverse generation, how long shall I be with you, and suffer you? Bring thy son hither. And as he was yet a coming, the devil threw him down, and tare him. And Jesus rebuked the unclean spirit, and healed the child, and delivered him again to his father.*

Things that happen in the spiritual world are often different from what is happening in the physical world. In deliverance, physically we cast out demons from a person's body. There was a case where a demon would easily get out of a person's body by just a word of Jesus' name, and that demon was just a lesser demon. Yet, when we face a powerful demon, we often struggle much in the physical just before we get the victory. In the Bible, we see Jesus casting out demons, even powerful ones by just a word, and there are some details of this listed. Jesus can easily cast out demons, and demons will not resist him, simply because he is full of power and faith, so much so that there is no ounce of doubt that lives in his mind. But when it comes to us, the case is different.   Strong resistance happens when doubt is present in the heart and mind of the victim, and sometimes in the deliverance team. This is true in the passage above in which both the father of the victim and the disciples had doubt in their heart and mind (Luke 9:40-41), that made the deliverance seem to fail. In some passages, the disciples asked Jesus privately why they were not able to cast the demons out, and Jesus told them to fast and pray, for this kind of demon can't easily be cast out by a weak faith. Some mistakenly understood Jesus' statement there and said, prayer and fasting would cast out powerful demons, but it is our faith that grows bigger every time we fast and pray that makes the powerful demons to be cast out without fail.

Crying, convulsing, foaming, rolling and strange movements in the deliverance

The crying, convulsing, and foaming are not the work of God, neither of the deliverance team, as often ignorant people say it is, but as the scripture says, it was the demons inside the body that cause those weird movements of the person's body (Luke 9:39, 42). This strange physical movement was not the work of the victim, the deliverance team, nor even by the Lord, but by the demons inside a person's body. It's like a snake that is being exposed to a fire; it will wiggle and roll and struggle much due to the heat of the fire. It will even try to find a way to run away from the fire to save itself, and this is the same with those that are demon-possessed. It's not their own work, but the work of the demons inside. There were times when the demons inside a person's body would make the person get their tongue outside of their mouth, and they would hiss like a snake, and sometimes crawl and roll on the ground. Also, in some events the victim's body was used to attack the deliverance team; that's why often we advise the persons in charge to bind the person with a rope/cloth so as to not hurt others or themselves. Often a demonized person will run out of the house naked, and the demons will even try to make the person to be hit by a car on a street. Every case is different. Sometimes their eyes would literally look like snakes' eyes! God in his grace trained and exposed us for years in a different kind of deliverance ministry, both on the inside of the church, and on the outside.

Scene in heaven

Matthew 16:19: *And I will give unto thee the keys of the kingdom of heaven: and whatsoever thou shalt bind on earth shall be bound in heaven: and whatsoever thou shalt loose on earth shall be loosed in heaven.*

Matthew 18:18-20: *Verily I say unto you, Whatsoever ye shall bind on earth shall be bound in heaven: and whatsoever ye shall loose on earth shall be loosed in heaven. Again I say unto you, That if two of you shall agree on earth as touching anything that they shall ask, it shall be done for them of my Father which is in heaven. For where two or three are gathered together in my name, there am I in the midst of them.*

In one of our experiences in a deliverance ministry, the Lord by his grace allowed some of our members to see the scene that took place in the spiritual world. While we were engaging the demons from a person's body, casting them out in Jesus' name (some victims used to have thousands or even millions of demons in their bodies, since demons are not subject to a physical limitation, a million can get inside and dwell in a person's body, and often this kind makes the person very violent and strong), in the heavens we were standing before them, fighting them in Jesus' name (sometimes with the assistance of angels), holding onto the golden sword of the Spirit, striking them very fast and powerfully! Our members saw us having our different kinds of golden armor and weapons. Once we defeat all the lesser demons, we at last face the leader, which makes the battle much more intense and serious than at first, when we were fighting the minions. In this book we listed the names of them given to us by God through a revelation. Often these leaders are backed up by Abaddon, Razum, and Nathan. It seems that God is allowing the battle to become harder and harder for the reason of us utilizing the gifts and power that he gave to us, and also to mold our hearts and minds to become persistent until the end. Of all the demons we fought, the spirit of unforgiveness is a little bit harder to be cast out, since we have to speak first to the person that was possessed by this demon, to forgive a person, so this demon will lose his ground inside them. Sometimes when the pain is deep, forgiveness seems like it is impossible, but nevertheless by the help of God, it is possible.

When we deal with the leader, we observe that the person is much more violent and strong; it is as if it just reserved its full strength for the last part of the battle. Often demons try to deceive the deliverance team by pretending that they are already cast out, but when we leave the house or the person, they will again get inside and possess that person (as long as there is an open door), and this time they will invite a much more powerful company, so as to strengthen their stronghold. That's why we make sure that the person has already being delivered by first talking to them and telling them to declare with their lips that Jesus is Lord. If the person resists saying that, it means the fight is not yet over. Demons can imitate the person's voice, movements, etc., but one thing for sure they will not do, and that is to declare that Jesus is Lord. Sometimes deliverance would be an overnight process, and this is tiresome. Since we are still in the flesh, our strength can be limited, and demons know this. So, they will resist to be cast out until the end just when they observe that we are losing our physical strength. Physical exhaustion can often pull down our minds and emotions, which will result in doubt. That's why we have to be persistent to deliver a person out of demonic oppression until the end, even if it is an overnight, or week-long deliverance! Once a demon senses our persistence, they lose their confidence and later on give up themselves, before they are totally tortured by us in Jesus' name. Once that person got delivered, the demon and its hosts in the spiritual realm would all be in chains (sometimes by the angels, and sometimes golden chains would appear instantly as we rendered them powerless in Jesus' name). At the moment of them being cast out, they are automatically dragged back into hell, and soon Satan crushes them into pieces. Deliverance is only harder, or ends up in failure, once a person by his own free will does not agree to be delivered. This is a case-by-case basis. Sometimes it is due to unforgiveness; sometimes the person loves sin more than God's righteousness (John3:18-19, Mark6:5-6). If this happens, we advise the family that takes care of the victim to express love to the victim, that in this way the person would come to their senses and escape the trap of the enemy.

The things that need to be delivered

Luke 9:41: *And Jesus answering said, O faithless and perverse generation, how long shall I be with you, and suffer you? Bring thy son hither.*

Faith is the key to unlock all of God's blessings, even his deliverance. In a deliverance, we see a picture of a person that is spiritually (even physically) in a prison cell of Satan, and is being oppressed by him in so many ways. In the Bible we read about people who were in this pitiful condition for years; a woman who couldn't stand upright for eighteen years (Luke 13:11), the boy that was seized by a spirit of convulsion since his childhood (Mark 9:20-21), and these biblical accounts are just two of the spiritual oppressions that can be seen in the physical body of the victim. There is also demonic oppression that affects only the mind (confusion, lunatic), and the emotions, and it is very serious when the evil spirit takes control over the spirit of a person. Whatever kind of demonic oppression a person has, God is still powerful enough to deliver them, if only they will have Jesus. We have to understand that in believing for deliverance, the person that is involved or victimized can be the one to have the faith to be delivered so as to believe in Jesus, or the relatives of the person, as in the case of the convulsing boy (his father went to Jesus to ask for a deliverance), the centurion (Matthew 8:5-13), the friends of the paralytic (Matthew 9:1-5), and so on. Faith is effectual every time it is directed to Jesus. It is man's opportunity of allowing God to move in his life.

Not all deliverance is successful. This may puzzle you, but that is true both in the scriptures, and nowadays. We encountered many events of deliverance that weren't successful, simply because of lack of faith from the victim, and their relatives. There was an instance where a person was easily delivered from an evil spirit, yet when we (the deliverance team) got home, days after the event, the evil spirit again went inside the victim's body/life, and again tortured him/her, and for a time this confused us. The question, "What went wrong?" arises in our minds. Yet God is merciful enough to educate us, that according to him the reason why a cast out evil spirit can go back into the person's life is because the entry point is still open; the evil spirit is still welcome in the person's life (Matthew 12:43-45), and the most alarming truth is that, once that evil spirit gets back inside of the person's life, it will invite seven much more powerful demons with him to secure his house (the person). Since faith in God is the key to unlock the power of the Spirit that will deliver us from Satan, likewise, lack of faith maybe is the failure of the victim, the relatives, and sometimes of the deliverance team, like the case of the convulsing boy (Luke 9:37-42). That is why, before one decides to undergo deliverance, or even to perform deliverance, a prayer of faith must be done first, for we are told not to go to a war unprepared, lest there would be a casualty.

The deliverance team, especially the leader, should be prepared enough so as to have no spot or blemish within him that an enemy could use against him or her. I remember a case that took place in one of the deliverances that we did. The one that did the deliverance was a woman pastor, and it seemed like it was successful, yet the devil left her a threat of exposing all of her evil works, her secret, unconfessed sins, so that she still hides in her spiritual closet today. That's why we have been told: *Brethren, if a man be overtaken in a fault, ye which are spiritual, restore such an one in the spirit of meekness; considering thyself, lest thou also be tempted.* (Galatians 6:1).

About prophecy

Its effect

1 Corinthians 14:3-5: *But he that prophesieth speaketh unto men to edification, and exhortation, and comfort. He that speaketh in an unknown tongue edifieth himself; but he that prophesieth edifieth the church. I would that ye all spake with tongues, but rather that ye prophesied: for greater is he that prophesieth than he that speaketh with tongues, except he interpret, that the church may receive edifying.*

Revelation 19:10: *And I fell at his feet to worship him. And he said unto me, See thou do it not: I am thy fellowservant, and of thy brethren that have the testimony of Jesus: worship God: for the testimony of Jesus is the spirit of prophecy.*

The message of God given through a prophecy is for the strengthening of the church, in comparison to speaking in tongues (without interpretation) which is for the edification of the speaker only. That is why speaking in tongues with interpretation is the same as prophecy, for its message can be understood by the church. Nowadays born-again churches are divided in their stand about this gift of prophecy. Some say, it is not effectual today, since the Bible is already complete. They say it although there is not a single verse that will prove it. The others still believe in prophecy, and thereby receive the benefit of it. If we will try to notice the effect of this ministry, it is for the church's edification, exhortation, and comfort. So, failing to acknowledge this ministry or gift is the same as a failure to receive the benefit.

Edification is "oikodome" in the Greek, and it means: concretely structured, building, and it suggests of forming strongly as a whole. If Satan is busy in his evil work dividing the church, the ministry of prophecy also must be active in forming the church as whole and firmly structured. Since the church is composed of different people, having many differences in language, what helps them be united is the ministry of prophecy. Even in the Old Testament, the Israelite people often fell into confusion (that leads to division) when there was no prophet to lead them to the Lord. But when God sent his servant, the solution was applied, and people became one.

In our church, we dealt with different kinds of problems. These led some of us into trouble and weakened their faith, and some were carried away by them. Yet when the word of prophecy was given to us, it had the power to really establish us. The word of God is powerful enough to remove all kinds of demonic works such as confusion, by way of revelation. That is why the Lord taught us to always seek him in prayer, and not to stop, until he gives us the word that we need to know and hear. That often comes by the word of prophecy.

Exhortation is "paraklesis" in Greek, and it means imploration. It is much more about the declaration of God's promises and power in his word. This is establishing the authority and power of God's word through prophecy in a way that the human mind couldn't resist. When the prophets of old, and even the prophets of the New Testament prophesied the message of God, people's faith was being established, and it was as if they became reunited with God in the Spirit. The word of prophecy led them back to God, like what had happened at the time of John the Baptist. John's ministry was the fulfillment of Elijah's ministry of spiritual restoration of Israel, for he was the Elijah that was to come. By the power of the Spirit of prophecy, Israel went back again to God, and was restored, and the Lord was pleased to bless them, instead of punishing them (Malachi 4:5-6). The word of prophecy can be likened to a spring rain on a dry land, bread to a hungry stomach, and a guide to the misled. How many discouraged people of God have been strengthened by the exhortation given to them by God, through his prophet? When I was just a young man in the church, and my knowledge of him was very little, every time I heard that a prophet was visiting our (former) church, I used to sit in front, and even to stand when an altar call was given, wishing to receive a gift (or a word) of prophecy from the Lord, and praise God, that most of the prophecies given to me have already taken place, even now. The preaching at the pulpit can only become powerful if it is anointed by God, or the person that speaks is anointed to preach, and this effect is the same with the word of prophecy.

Comfort is "paramuthia" in Greek, and it means consolation. A church that is experiencing trouble after trouble is often misled and is confused, and if the leader lacks God's wisdom, he may tend to do things that instead of helping them, cause (much) trouble in the church, and this happened many times to the Israelite people in the Old Testament (Isaiah 30:1-3). That happened due to lack of discretion on behalf of their leader. Once their leader rejected God by not consulting him through his prophet, they experienced catastrophe, and the major casualty was destruction of their temple! But when the church has a wise leader that is yielding to the Spirit of God so as to pray first and wait for an answer before they do things, or to even seek for the word that will come directly from God, this brings them into the office of his servant, the prophet. Churches, even ministers, don't consult God through his prophet for so many reasons, but this is to their hurt. For a prophet is the eye and the ear of God in the church. The church of Smyrna managed to overcome their tribulations by having an ear that was willing to listen to the word of prophecy given to them by God through John the beloved (Revelation 2:8-11), until God made them to finish the race, and thereby they received their reward. Likewise nowadays, if churches, even ministers, have an ear to listen and a heart that is yielding to God so as to seriously look for the word of prophecy, they will really overcome all obstacles that they are now experiencing, and not just that, but as Jesus said, they will be able to do more miraculous things than he did.

My first personal testimony of this happened when I was in the Bible school. One of my classmates, who was just a young pastor at that time, was experiencing trouble in his ministry that was forcibly entrusted to him by his former discouraged pastor. We prayed that night, then suddenly God (I wasn't aware that it was a word of prophecy) gave me a word, and that word was three instructions that he was to apply so as to overcome his trouble. I still remember the instructions. They were as follows:

First, he was to not worry about of all the problems, but rather, lay them all down to the Lord.

 Second, he was to focus on evangelism, and,

third, he also had to reconcile the leaders (for there was division that was taking place among the leaders during that time, and he just shared it after I gave the word to him).

When he applied the instructions, breakthrough happened extraordinarily, and it took six weeks for him to have them all resolved, praise God! This is just one of the blessings that we can have if only we will acknowledge the ministry of prophecy in the church.

Its nature

2 Peter 1:20-21: *Knowing this first, that no prophecy of the scripture is of any private interpretation. For the prophecy came not in old time by the will of man: but holy men of God spake as they were moved by the Holy Ghost.*

In comparison to preaching and teaching, prophecy is a message given directly by God through the prophet to his people. Often preaching and teaching is a message given to us by way of man's understanding of the scripture, and we call it interpretation. However, prophecy is not, and must not be man's own interpretation (2 Peter 1:20-21), although we are to discern it for the sake of not being misled by the seducing spirits that twist the ministry of prophecy. Its message sometimes is just for an individual, and sometimes for the church.

The message

Like the theme and purpose of every message, both from the Bible, and at the pulpit, prophecy likewise has a different meaning for the person that will receive the message. Sometimes, the prophet has no relation with the recipient of the message, and sometimes they have, nevertheless, both are to understand that they are dealing not with their own words, but the word from above, and that they must take it seriously, for often failure to respond to God's message leads to grievous consequences.

Rebuke

Revelation 3:19: *As many as I love, I rebuke and chasten: be zealous therefore, and repent.*

God as a loving father to his children doesn't want them to be destroyed. Therefore, he gave them his law so that they may learn to live a life that is far away from sin. Sin, however, is deadly (Romans 5:21, 1 Corinthians 15:56), and God is faithful enough to protect us, his children, from death (spiritual). Throughout the story of the Bible, God often sends his message of rebuke toward his people, not just because he was angry, but because he loves them and does not want them to perish. We read the life of king Saul, the first king of Israel. When he began to disobey God, he was rebuked by the Lord through prophet Samuel, and that was to restore him, yet king Saul remained stubborn in that he wanted to please his men rather than his God (1 Samuel 15:22-24), and the consequence was fatal (1 Chronicles 10:13-14).

Praise/promotion

Revelation 3:8-11: *I know thy works: behold, I have set before thee an open door, and no man can shut it: for thou hast a little strength, and hast kept my word, and hast not denied my name. Behold, I will make them of the synagogue of Satan, which say they are Jews, and are not, but do lie; behold, I will make them to come and worship before thy feet, and to know that I have loved thee. Because thou hast kept the word of my patience, I also will keep thee from the hour of temptation, which shall come upon all the world, to try them that dwell upon the earth. Behold, I come quickly: hold that fast which thou hast, that no man take thy crown.*

God in his righteousness knows how to punish the unrighteous, even after so many times of giving them a chance to repent, and to reward the faithful according to his word. Right now, many have failed to come up into this knowledge of God, so that they often claim God's promise without looking at his word. The condition is that the promise requires obedience. The Philadelphian church, due to their faithfulness to God in spite of their hardships, was being praised by Jesus, and he promised to promote them by giving them an open door that no one could shut. That door of promotion made them able to defeat the Jews that falsely claimed to be servants of God, yet were not. Jesus promised them that those people would bow down before them as a gesture of defeat. That open door also gave them a grace that would enable them to be saved from the hour of temptation that would come upon all the world (both believers and unbelievers), while the others (even believers that go into carnality) will stumble and fall. Often this kind of trial is in the form of disasters, famine, plague, even war. In the Old Testament, leaders, judges, kings, prophets, priests, and even nations received God's promotion just when they responded to God's message. Nineveh was forgiven when they responded to God's message, yet Sodom and Gomorrah were both destroyed! David was promoted, while king Saul and the kings like him were all demoted, even their households. As the word of Daniel says: *He removes kings, and appoints kings* (Daniel 2:21).

Warning

Mathew 24:37-39: *But as the days of Noe were, so shall also the coming of the Son of man be. For as in the days that were before the flood they were eating and drinking, marrying and giving in marriage, until the day that Noe entered into the ark, And knew not until the flood came, and took them all away; so shall also the coming of the Son of man be.*

The message of warning can be given to both faithful and unfaithful, like the story of Noah and the flood. Jesus mentioned it to his disciples and to the world (for it is part of the gospel) as a sign of his coming, and also as a warning to all. At Noah's time, people were very busy with their physical business (eating, drinking, marrying, and giving in marriage) so as not to listen to the preaching of Noah about the flood. According to the book of Jasher, Noah built the ark with his sons for five years, and preached about the flood to people at his time up to one hundred and twenty years, until they went into the ark, and food came in. The righteous man Noah was warned by God, and because he believed God, he and his family were saved, yet the world that received the same message of warning perished. Israel also, with its king and its noble men, was warned by God through Jeremiah the prophet of the upcoming destruction from the hand of the Babylonian king. This was a result of their disobedience to his word, and the only way for them to escape this was to surrender to the foreign wicked king that later on was punished by God, and repented, and was saved. Yet even after years of hearing the message from Jeremiah, the king rejected it, and so the noblemen even physically mistreated the prophet that sent them the message. They fooled themselves by believing that peace and safety shall be coming after them, yet the truth was it was a sword of the enemy! Therefore, because of their disobedience, Israel's wall and gates were burned, its temple was crushed, and the people were killed, and some were brought into Babylon as captives for seventy years (Jeremiah 29:10). This same message of warning is still effectual nowadays. In our church, God tested us in this message one step at a time. Since he promised to not give us a temptation that is too heavy for us to bear, he in his wisdom was using little things to train us, to see whether we would obey or disobey. One after another of warning messages were given to us by the Lord. Some had a physical consequence only; some affected us spiritually.

On one occasion, God warned the young people of our church to be holy and to remove all worldly songs, pictures, and movies from their cell phones. Yet, after so many warnings, the youth still went on in their lives playing with satanic songs, pictures etc. Then one day, it happened. The Lord's punishment to them was that he destroyed all of their cellphones! Yes, all their cellphones! When this happened, they had mixed thoughts about it: just a coincidence, or a punishment? This kind of experience happens to us in a different manner. Sometimes the consequence of disobedience of a warning was physical sickness, sometimes loss of valuable things, sometimes an accident, and the greatest was physical or untimely death! If only we people of God will learn to obey God, great things will happen like of old, and much more shall be given to us by the Lord.

The message of warning to other Christian churches

In the letter of prophet Jeremiah, chapter 49, he was given a message of warning to be given to other nations that surround Israel. The prophecy was for the nations of Ammon, Edom, Kedar, and Elam. The Lord was giving them a warning to repent, lest like Israel, they too would fall into the sword of punishment. Sadly, all of them, like Israel, repented after the punishment was done, due to their stubbornness!

Our church also, since God gave us a prophetic ministry (by fire), was given a message of warning to be given to different Christian churches here in our place at Laguna. The message of warning was due to spiritual adultery and the sin of idolatry which were committed by many professing Christian churches here in our place. Some were serving a god of mammon, some serve for the sake of pleasing men, some for material gain, etc., and those churches (even now) were having a wealthy physical condition, like the Sardis and Laodicean churches. We, in obedience to God, sent his message of warning to these churches, and as we expected, all of them rejected the message. The message was for them to repent, by walking again into the path of the spirit, and seeking God's holiness, righteousness, and power by means of praying and fasting, and totally leaving the ways of men. One of the bishops here in Laguna was warned by the Lord that he was being like pharaoh to his people! He was dominating them and leading them away from God. He was forcing them, even threatening them, by imputing fear into their hearts if they disobeyed him, as if they were disobeying the Lord himself. When I gave this message to this bishop (he knows me), he rejected the message, and acted as if we were attacking him. I told him to ask his prophets to discern the message, to see if it was from God or not, yet he wasn't willing to, lest his work would be exposed. He even asked me to give him a message of praise, and I remembered king Saul's hypocrisy when he was rebuked by prophet Samuel; he asked the prophet to honor him before people, even though he knew that he was under God's rebuke! Like king Saul, as a result of his disobedience, God removed this man (the bishop) from him (John 15:2,6). Visions of demons swamping into his church were given on different occasions. Every time, we plead mercy for him, and for others. Physically, like the others, they are at the pulpit preaching the message, and are even able to travel from one place to another so as to pretend to be a servant of God, yet in the spirit they are already cut off, and are now dying (spiritually). People like them are often killed by Satan through car accidents, plane crashes, and whatsoever means he uses to kill them untimely. Truly, the words of Hebrews 10:30-31 are true: *For we know him who said, "Vengeance is mine; I will repay." And again, "The Lord will judge his people." It is a fearful thing to fall into the hands of the living God.*

Instructions

Psalm 32:8: *I will instruct thee and teach thee in the way which thou shalt go: I will guide thee with mine eye.*

Each and every day of our life in this world is often occupied by the things of the world. Yet, we are being told to always walk by the Spirit, and to let the Spirit of God lead us all the way through our journey with Christ until we reach the end. Great men and women of God were all able to finish their races victoriously, simply because they all had this one thing in common: They followed God's instructions.

Church members' testimonies

Sister April Joy

I am April Joy Platilla, and am praising God for this great opportunity that he gave me, and also gave to us, to testify of his goodness to our life; how he saved us, and how he uses us for his glory. I'm 26 years old now by the grace of God, and am now temporarily working in one of the department stores at Los Banos, Laguna, so as to help my husband in finances until the time when God's promised provision will come, that we can be able to go in the full-time ministry. My family came from a Roman Catholic religion and were once idol worshippers, yet by the grace and mercies of God, we are now saved from that idolatrous lifestyle, that will end up in hell. My first encounter with going to the born-again church happened when I was invited the first time at the church's anniversary by my friend, who is a believer of Christ. I observed immediately the differences in the style of worship that I used to know in my former religion, when I got inside their church. The place seemed filled with joy and celebration, and some presentation of singing to the Lord. After the worship celebration there was eating, and we went home. It happened when I met my boyfriend, who is now my husband, the servant of the Lord, pastor Joven, and he invited me to attend their church worship (he wasn't yet a pastor at that time), and I accepted the invitation simply because he was my boyfriend. When we got into their church, I observed that people were singing a song of worship to the Lord while their hands were lifted up, and some were crying. I thought, "What is this?" Since the first church that I attended was celebrating, and now this one was crying, I later on understood that this was what we call intense worship. We decided even at the early times of our knowing each other to marry each other informally (without a legal wedding ceremony). Since pastor Joven was studying still in the Bible school during that time (from

Tuesday to Friday), I was left alone in their house, and that happened for two years, and at that time my encounter with the Lord happened by me listening to gospel music day by day as my way to comfort myself while the pastor was gone. Every time I listened to the song of worship, it seemed like it was speaking to me, and that I was hearing the Lord talking gently to me. Every message of the songs spoke directly to my heart, and I was touched deeply! This spiritual encounter from the Lord through the gospel music went on until we decided to begin our every night prayer meeting in our house, and my knowledge of the Lord went deeper every time I sought him in prayer and in his word. The Lord helped me understand the message that pastor Joven shared to me about Jesus, and this made me to really believe him to be my Lord and Savior, and thus I decided to fully surrender my life to him. He led me to really know him, and each and every day I was having this deep hunger of knowing him the way that my former religion couldn't do for me. I fell in love with the Lord day by day, and the desire to share/preach him to others burns in my heart. One of the miracles that the Lord had done to us was when he healed my sister Bernadette of her long-time rheumatic heart. I invited her into one of our prayer meetings, and then Prophetisa (pastor Joven's mom) was used by the Lord to pray over her and declare healing upon my sister. She also saw in a vision of the little dark spot on my sister's heart, even though no one told her about her rheumatic heart. After the meeting, she shared it to our mother, and they confirmed it by going on to their doctor, and the doctor was amazed by the result of the x-ray, for not seeing the spot on her heart, and she was declared healed! Hallelujah!

I was greatly encouraged by this miraculous healing, so that I really worked hard to preach Jesus, even to my mother and brothers (we are a broken family, and my father already had abandoned us by having another family). By the goodness of the Lord I managed to bring my entire family to him in just a matter of years, and our life was filled with the blessings of the Lord and this also led me to preach him to my friend as he led me.

Little by little the Lord molds me, by changing my mindset, my emotions, and even my desires. He taught me to be contented with the little things that have, yet drove me to always seek him daily and be filled with his Spirit. Now, I am serving the Lord in a worship ministry, leading the church in worship songs, and also, I preach Christ to my workmates in such a way that some of them decided to follow Christ like me. I give all the honor and glory to Christ Jesus alone! Hallelujah!

Brother Jeff

I'm Jeffrey Mendoza, and was blessed by the Lord God almighty with the spiritual name of "Soldier of God." In 2013 I was a salesman, and at my work I met Brother Daniel Bacalso, who was one of my co-workers and also was a member of the Christ the Living Word Fire Ministry at that time. He is kind and generous, and he used to preach the word of God to me daily while we were at work. At first, I was confused and seemed to understand nothing. I understood later that it's because my mind was blinded with the worldly things, so that the word of God couldn't take its place inside my mind and heart. But because of his persistent witnessing to me of the word of God, it happened that it really sank into my heart and mind, and I was captured by it. Daniel invited me to join their fellowship, and in that fellowship, I met pastor Joven Platilla, and the brethren. He prayed for me that night, and he even told me to fully surrender my life to Jesus Christ and serve him. I was filled with vices; alcohol, cigarettes, and sometimes I was a trouble maker, and I found myself that night being prayed for by the servant of the Lord. Pastor Joven shared to me the gospel about the love of God that he showed when he sent Jesus on a cross to die for the sins of mankind. Led by the Holy Spirit, I decided to surrender my life to Jesus at that time, and prayed for forgiveness and acceptance of the Lord Jesus Christ. When the man of God laid his hand upon me to pray, I felt power and wonderful peace fall upon me, so that I burst into tears. I experienced the forgiveness of God, and the freedom of my soul from all the burdens of sin. I also felt something hot that filled my head and body - something like powerful (holy) fire, and this made my body start sweating, and at the same time I felt like I was floating into the air; I felt like I was a new man inside! That night of having fellowship with them continues on until now, and I praise God for that encounter! I totally committed my life to the Lord as I continually attended our gatherings in the church. I, like pastor Joven and his family, and the church members, used to follow God's instructions even when he led us to transfer and go on full-time with him at barangay Sucol Calamba Laguna. At that place we had been commanded by the Lord to give up everything; even our work, and also our earthly desires. It wasn't that easy at first. We gave up everything from this world, things that we think are very important so that they even make us to forget our Creator, just to have them! At that place God took away from us everything; cell phones, our friends, our evil habits, and even our burden on the family, in exchange for a total commitment to him, and for the spiritual training that he did to us for two years. We had truly experienced Matthew 6:33 at that place during those years. We happened to even go to the lakeshore to catch fish for food, and even tried to ask fishermen at that place to give us some of their catch. At that place God opened our spiritual senses so as to behold the spiritual realm. I really experienced what it meant to really trust God in everything at that place of spiritual training. In exchange for our obedience to God's call for this training of losing everything for his sake, and the gospel, the Lord allowed us to receive power beyond measure. I personally experienced casting a demon out from a person's body during those years; a thing that I learned wasn't common to all Christians. I learned later on that not all Christians have this kind of encounter (casting out demons) even after attending the church for many years for so many reasons; reasons that are not enough to deny the promised signs of power by the Lord to those that will believe in him (Mark 16:17). Aside from the experience of deliverance, the Lord allowed us, and even I, to be attacked by demons in so many ways, and one was through a nightmare! Pastor Joven taught us day by day how to battle the enemy and defeat him by faith in Jesus' name, and by using the power and gifts that the Holy Spirit gave us. My heart and mind were both captured by the Lord that he made me to seek him day by day and forget the world at the same time. We also have been attacked by Satan at that place, even by him using our stomachs and minds. Since we all are full-time, and we were almost twenty adults and ten children at that place that have to be fed, and yet we have not even 10,000 pesos (an amount that is good only for five to six people as a regular allowance monthly, according to one of the surveys) in our church's budget monthly, yet by the grace of God we overcame, praise God! Truly God sustains us miraculously in so many different ways day by day. As he provided to prophet Elijah by an angel, a crow, and a widow; God also provided for us without fail. He uses different persons, and different ways to sustain us so that we may learn to only trust in him, and to become flexible and survivors in all circumstances that he gives to us. There were lots of spiritual experiences that we have had at that place, until the Lord moved us into another place at Bay Laguna, and now at Los Banos Laguna. At this time, I am already married to one of our church mates, and we both are serving the Lord on our place at Bulihan Quezon, preaching the gospel to my family, and sometimes to the family of my wife (Analyn) at Guinyangan Quezon. The power of the Lord upon us is mighty enough to save our family, and this made me to really continue serving God, for I know that he is faithful to all of his promises. All praise and honor belong to God alone!

Sister Analyn

I am humbled and blessed by the Lord for giving me the spiritual name "Clean Water." In October 2013, I first met the Lord Jesus and I decided to surrender my life to him at that time, and my life was changed supernaturally from that time and forward. I was a former employee of SM Calamba Laguna. From that place of work, I met the servant of the Lord who is now my husband, Brother Jeffrey Mendoza. He was assigned to train me at work, and that was the beginning of us being close to each other, until such a time that he little by little shared to me the word of God. Brother Jeff used to encourage me every time I was down, by teaching me the word of God. I used to live like the waves of the sea; tossed to and fro, and my life had no sure direction of a good future, until the Lord found me. I used to believe and behave like the purpose in this life is only for the sake of worldly pleasures, that as long as you are happy in doing things, and that you don't mistreat others, that is what we really need to have so as to fulfill our life's mission; yet I found out that I was greatly wrong in this. Brother Jeff patiently trained me about our work, and also the word of God, until he decided to invite me to attend one of the prayer meetings of the Christ the Living Word Church. At that place I met pastor Joven Platilla, his wife, sister April Joy, Mama Propetisa, and the brethren. The first time that I went into that place/church, I felt something wonderful inside of me for that place. It was as if the place was telling me, "You are very welcome here, and this is the place and people to whom you really belong!" The brethren welcomed me with all of their hearts and made me feel at ease, as if I was really family to them. I also don't want to miss to share to you that the place wasn't good physically; it was an old type house; some called it a haunted house (the oldest house at that place), and it was dark inside, having only some light with gas in it to lighten the whole house. The house seemed like it was ugly and gloomy in the physical, yet it is glorious and filled with God's presence on the inside! This is a place that an ordinary man wouldn't choose to be his dwelling place, since people look and evaluate everything on the outside; therefore, they often miss God and his blessings that are spiritual, and can't just be perceived using our physical knowledge. That night, after the worship service, pastor Joven spent time to talk to me, and led me to really give up my worldly life so as to receive a new life from the Lord. He said to me, "Offer God your life and body as a living sacrifice," and he will use it for his glory. The pastor led me to lay down all my burdens to the Lord in our prayer. I laid down my personal desires, my family, and all of my problems in prayer, and while I was praying for this, I felt something powerful manifest in me and take all the burdens inside of me, so that I really felt I was free from all of those heavy burdens! That night I decided to surrender all my life to Jesus Christ, and promised to serve him only. While the pastor was praying for me, laying his hand on me, I felt the power of God all over my body, so that it had me shaking gently. I couldn't understand what was happening at that time; all I know was that I felt complete, safe, and secure in God. I praise God for that experience of freedom from all of my worries and fears in this life. Now, I and brother Jeff serve the Lord at their place by starting to build a small church there. We are there, patiently serving the Lord while waiting for his promises to happen. I give all the glory and praise to our dear Lord Jesus Christ.

Sister Riza

I am Rizalie Castillo, now 26, and I surrendered my life to the Lord Jesus when sister April (Pastor Joven's wife) shared with me the good news of salvation. We at that time were both working at a department store as sales clerks. I was convicted by the Lord and found myself repenting of my sins, even though at first it sounded weird, yet I experienced the power of God touching my heart like never before. I, like the other sinners, used to live a life of sin:

drinking alcohol and smoking, without my parents' knowledge. But my life began to change after I experienced the love of God, and his power led me to throw away all the evil things that I used to do. My heart and mind were filled with the peace of God, and knowledge of him made me to understand everything day by day, that God has a purpose for everything, even for my life. We came from a poor family, and our parents died untimely. The loss of them made us siblings to live with difficulty, yet now I understand that for all those years the Lord never left us. The presence of the Lord inside of me made me to know him more. The thoughts of knowing him and his word made me to feel complete, and all the worries and fears were gone. I decided to attend the fellowships and began to commit myself in the ministry. Sister April exerted so much effort to invite me to the fellowships, and every time I was there, I felt at ease and comfortable. The Lord allowed my little faith to be tested by circumstances. One day when we attended a church gathering, I lost my ID, and this might mean that I wouldn't be able to go into my work unless I had it. In this I was a little bit troubled, but the Lord spoke to me through sister April by saying, "Don't you worry; you will have it later," then suddenly a thought came into my mind that it was in the guard's office. After the fellowship I immediately went into our working place, then the guard asked for my ID, then suddenly another guard appeared and gave me my ID. This little good thing made me to be amazed by the Lord's kindness. I continued attending fellowship with sister April and met lots of the brethren. New things from the Lord filled my life as I decided to follow the Lord, and the old things of my life were gone one by one. I even surrendered my boyfriend, since he was an unbeliever, and later on I learned that he had gotten married one month after our break up. This hurt me, but the Lord strengthened me.

One of the amazing things that I had from the Lord happened when we were attending an all-night prayer meeting together with pastor

Joven, his family, and some of our friends. In this prayer meeting the Lord allowed us to experience a supernatural event: seeing heaven and hell and battling with demons using the power of God. I also learned different kinds of satanic works against serious Christians, and we were being taught by pastor Joven to fight them back. The Lord gave me a word of promise that empowers my spirit. Words like, "You are like a royal diadem in the hands of your mighty God," and, "You will no longer be called, 'forsaken', but you will be called, a delight to God, and a bride to him". This made me to realize God's unfailing love for me. I'm happy that the Lord chose me to be his. In spite of my sins, still he loves me. His love for me made me to really seek him, and physical exhaustion couldn't stop me from attending our all-night prayer meeting. The brethren and I had an unlimited spiritual and physical strength because of the power of God. Most of us worked during the day, then went to the fellowship after we had our dinner. We did this Monday through Friday. The Lord changed my heart and my mind - he taught me to fix my eyes on things above; to always believe in the unseen things that are in his word. He even taught me to set my hope on heaven since everything in this world is just temporary. I praise the Lord that he even taught me to understand his word, and to have the power to preach it to others. Right now, I'm one of his servants, serving him at Christ the Living Word church led by pastor Joven. All honor and glory belong to him alone. Amen.

Sister Christina

I'm Christina Magalona, called to serve him here unto eternity, amen. I used to know the Lord only in mind before. Yet, he made himself known to me by allowing the enemy to strike my son with asthma, and this made him to be in the hospital weekly, and this also made us fall into a huge debt. My husband was a professing believer, yet during those times I couldn't see any fruit of his faith, and sadly I'd never even heard him calling on the name of the Lord. During those times of difficulty, I didn't know where to run for help. I even prayed to God that I would do anything, if only he would heal my son. God's answer came to me the day when our new neighbor (pastor Joven) and his family had their Sunday worship service in their rental house, which was just next door to ours. At first, I just observed and listened to their fellowship, especially to the message that was preached powerfully by the pastor; it really struck my heart. It was as if the Lord was talking to me! It was as if I was awakened from my deep sleep. I couldn't explain the wonderful experience that I had the first time that I heard and received the word of God. I was filled with wonderful peace. The next Sunday, I decided to attend and join them at their worship service, although at first, I was a little bit shy, and this was the beginning of the breakthrough in my life. I learned a lot the time that I was with them. Things like: I'm not supposed to ask God for everything I want; I also must learn to serve him, and that I also have to deny my sinful nature in order to follow Jesus. I used to sleep, eat, buy and do things as I wanted, but now I was taught to only do the will of God, and I love these changes. It was as if every time I do them, it brings me peace to my soul. I understand that as a believer in Christ, I should no longer live in this body, but Christ should live in me. The Lord changed my heart, mind, emotions, and even actions gradually. I learned to read the Bible, and pray daily, and even to pray in the middle of the night. My life is not complete if I don't pray. One of the mysterious things that happened every time I prayed was that tears flowed down my cheeks overwhelmingly. My mind used to wonder why my tears were falling down naturally, especially when I was in my deep prayer. Later on, pastor Joven explained to me that the Lord called me to be a weeping prophet, and with that the Lord gave me a spiritual name: "Weeping Woman." The Lord miraculously healed my son, and little by little helped us to pay our debt, and get out of it. Wonderful things happened normally as I continued to follow the Lord. The Lord answered my prayers for my family, and even for others, without fail. Right now, I am serving the Lord at Christ the Living Word church as an intercessor. I praise the almighty God for all of the great things that he has done, and keeps on doing to me, and to my family (I also began to evangelize my siblings and other relatives in spite of the persecution, yet we are bringing them to Christ one by one). Truly God is alive and is faithful to his word. All honor and glory belong to God alone, in Jesus' name, amen.

Sister Bernadette

I'm Bernadette Marasigan, and I only want to testify of the Lord's power to heal. I used to have a rheumatic heart, and this made our mother spend most of her money buying the medicine, and paying the doctor's bills, that there were times she had to even borrow from her employer. This illness used to make me suffer physically, even when I was a child. I couldn't play with other children because of this, and even when I was a teenager, I wasn't allowed to do things that would trigger this illness, and this made me feel incomplete. I used to live life apart from Jesus. We came from a Catholic faith, and this faith does us no good. Before, I thought that life is all about having good clothing, eating delicious food, and having fun with my friends. We used to go inside the Catholic chapel every Sunday just because of our mother. She was a devout Catholic until she became a believer by the passionate prayer and witnessing of our elder sister April Joy (pastor Joven's wife). I was much too attracted to people that were very passionate about their physical appearance, yet when I became a believer this was changed. I used to just call on the name of the Lord with my lips only, and during the times that I was in difficulty, but I had no commitment to him. My encounter with the Lord happened when I was invited by my sister April to attend their prayer meeting. Compared to the Catholics that gather at a huge chapel with many sculptures and images, we happened to gather at their house - no images of saints, and no sculptures. Her husband preached the gospel to us, and the message sank thoroughly into my heart. I ended up surrendering my life to Jesus in a prayer. One of the striking events that took place that night, was when the pastor's mom (Prophetisa) prayed with me for healing of the rheumatic heart, and this was without my informing her of my illness. I was surprised then, and she even told me that my heart has a small black spot in it, and that was exactly true. She prayed for healing, and suddenly I felt the power of God, and I was healed that night of my long-time illness, and this miracle made our mom also believe in the Lord, because she also used to suffer with me in this illness. She, like me and my two brothers, surrendered her life to Jesus. The doctor confirmed my healing and stopped the medication. This really is the evidence that Jesus is alive and is powerful. I praise the almighty God for his healing power.

Brother Salvador

I'm 36, and lived at San Pablo Laguna. We lived a miserable life. We are the only two children of our parents, and our father lived having many vices: gambling, drinking, etc. Our mom went abroad to work, and we ended up living a life far away from God. Like our father I had vices - drinking, taking drugs, women, and had been involved with robbery. During those times of doing those evil things, I felt empty deep inside of me. The alcohol, women, and drugs couldn't fill the emptiness I felt within. Every time I recognized it, it seemed to go deeper. One day I asked myself, "Is this really the purpose of my life? Is this what I want?" Then, I realized that I had begun to cry. I was crying like a child, looking for the purpose of my life, and that made me realize that there is God in heaven, and I began to call upon the name of Jesus, and repented of my sins. I literally confessed all my sins that I could remember, and I heard the Lord telling me, "You are forgiven; go and sin no more!" The Lord allowed me to meet Brother Daniel. We both worked in the same place; I am one of the security guards, and he is a messenger there. He testified to me about Jesus, and even invited me to attend their fellowship, and I gave in. I met pastor Joven at the fellowship, and I was awakened spiritually by the message he shared to us that night! I had been a believer already, but went on to backsliding, and my faith had dried up. This happened because of the problem that arose in our former church. At pastor Joven's church, I was refreshed and was restored by the Lord. My mind was renewed and my heart was healed of all the worries and fears, and the fire that had died begin to rekindle in my spirit. The Lord gave me excitement again to attend a fellowship, and even now I attend our weekly fellowship at Christ the Living Word Church, and I also began to preach Christ to others. The Lord also led me to throw away all my evil habits as a testimony to his power. In addition to this, my daughter, my wife, and my parents all now believe the Lord, and this, too, is one of his answers to my prayers, and this made me to really serve him, whatsoever will happen. All the glory belongs to God alone, in Jesus' name.

Sister Vilma

So much thanks to our gracious Lord for the privilege of sharing my living testimony of how he showed his unfailing love for me, and to my family, even at the times that I almost gave up in following him. Due to financial crisis I decided to work abroad in Kuwait for two years and four months. I am a widow who had to take care of my daughters and my family's needs. When I went to Kuwait I also was struggling spiritually. As a single mom, I longed for a companion. This made me to have a wrong relationship with an unbeliever, and as a result I suffered condemnation from other Christians from my former church.

Having this, I tried to escape from them, and my way of doing that was to work outside the country. In Kuwait, I also suffered with the unfair treatment of our employer. He didn't comply with the written contract, as many of us OFW's used to experience, even not giving me a day off. I suffered much spiritually and physically, and for all those times I tried to survive by reading the Bible and prayer, and yet even after having these, I felt emptiness inside. I was yearning for the presence of God. As I was praying, God answered me unexpectedly, and that was by the live preaching that appeared on my Facebook wall. My spiritual hunger and thirst were met by the message being preached by the live streaming ministry of the man of God, none other than pastor Joven. When I listened to him, it was like a spring of water that sprung up in my heart, that is continuously flowing even now, and this was the beginning of my breakthrough. I decided, as the Lord led me, to watch pastor's live preaching on Facebook daily. I was filled spiritually, and my spirit was healed and was restored by God as I went on watching this young man's ministry. God enlightened me, and the trouble in my heart was resolved. Questions have been answered, and my heart was motivated to follow God more than before. My former pastor was once a spiritual person that was dedicated to the work of God. He was passionately serving the Lord, until he got involved with false teachings that were embraced by him. This is the G12 system. From being spiritual, his life and preaching became focused on the physical things. The message at the pulpit was always about money, and the growth of the numbers of church members, and this made our spiritual wall to collapse in the spirit that made us to be unprotected against our enemies. Many know this, but no one would dare to question the pastor's decision, for if they did, they would be marked as rebellious sheep. They sow fear in the hearts of the congregations. Different kinds of teachings were made, just to make the members give their money to the church, so as to prove their obedience. One false teaching that they created is the teaching of "giving the first fruit". In this teaching, they are encouraging us to give the entire first salary to the church by faith, without thinking where to get your allowance the next time you go into your workplace. This created confusion in the family, for this seemed like suicide! Yet they call it faith, and even clap their hands for those that obey, and put pressure on those that are unwilling. In their system, a simple member couldn't easily approach our former pastor to talk to him. He is now a bishop. This is different from Jesus, who always loved to be with the poor, even the children. If you want to talk to the pastor, you have to talk to your cell group leader first, and we also were prohibited from having fellowship with some of our brethren that were in a different cell group, so as (according to them) to avoid division and disorder.

When I began to follow pastor Joven's preaching, things began to change gradually, yet powerfully. Praise God for his life. Through the wisdom given to him from above, all my spiritual confusion, struggling, and questions have been enlightened, and most of all, I was challenged to get out of my comfort zone. I also was being delivered from my evil habits, and was now being used by God to help others by encouragement. Not just that, the Lord also confirmed my calling of being his servant to lead his people through the prophecy and wisdom given to me by his humble servant. Now I decided to begin my new spiritual journey with the Lord as his servant, beginning inside my household, and to some people that are looking for God's touch in their lives. All the glory and honor belong to God alone! Hallelujah!

Brother Ruben

February 14, 2014, the first time I went to Saudi Arabia to work as an OFW, my mind was captured by the things of the flesh. Though I was a Christian, I bore no fruit for my faith. I had a dead faith in Christ. I only knew him in word, but my heart and mind were both fixed on earthly things only, and I thought that it was just fine. I became like those who have a form of godliness and yet deny its power. In my daily living I denied the power of the cross. I denied not myself, but Jesus, and I thought that was just fine. I had no time with the word of God, very rarely did I pray, and often my prayers were self-centered and contained only my fleshly desires, which I now understand were abominable to the Lord. Days, weeks, months, and even years passed by as I was living as a carnal Christian, and this made me feel empty. Worldly things lead to emptiness; that's what I understand. It was as if I was a slave to my flesh, and I couldn't stop it from dragging me into doing evil things. I was hopeless, I was powerless, yet I knew that I was a Christian then. I understand the message of Paul when he said, "The things I am doing are not the ones that I wanted to do, rather, I am doing what I hate, and wretched man that I am, who can save me from this body of sin?" Praise Jesus– he is my salvation! He made a way for me!

The Lord in his mercy provided a way of escape from this dungeon of hell. God convicted me of my sins, and I repented. I begged for his mercy to forgive me, and give me the power to overcome the works of the flesh. I experienced the Lord's mighty hand lifting me up, taking me out of the muddy place of sin. The Lord again gave me the desire and the power to do his great pleasure. I was again living as a believer that serves him with all my heart. I again delighted myself in the Lord by reading his word, and by prayer. My first contract as a worker in Saudi Arabia ended, and I again, by the mercies of the Lord, was given another chance to go back working abroad. It was just like another day, as it was before. The emptiness that I felt was still present in me, and there was an urge in me to satisfy it. The feeling was like I need to find something, and I need to seek it until I find it, because if not, I was sure that I would again go back to the life of sin that I had already repented of, and this time would be much worse than it was before. I prayed, and sought God for an answer, and God in his mercy provided me the answer. It's true that if only we will ask the Lord for his will to be done, that he will grant it without delay. His answer came this way: one day I was scrolling on Facebook, then suddenly it popped up - the live streaming of a young pastor. He was preaching powerfully enough that his message caught my entire being, and I listened to his preaching for more than an hour!

I even found myself crying and repenting of my sins, with tears flowing down on my cheeks, and I was like a hungry and thirsty baby that longs for milk, which is the word of God. His message satisfied my long-time craving, and it was as if I didn't want it to end. It's a mystery how I found his live streaming video, since we don't know each other, but one thing is for sure, God led me to him. I decided to follow his live streaming, watching for it daily. The message was always striking, and it really shook my being. At the end of it the conclusion was always: "Yes Lord, yes Lord, I will follow you!" I was challenged to really lay down my life to the Lord and serve him! Yes, serve him! This is one thing that I greatly missed as a believer; serving the Lord with all my heart, mind, soul, and body, and now that I have found it, I will not fail to do it. I at this time dedicated my life to serve the Lord, by following the live streaming of this pastor, and also commit to support his ministry financially, and I praise God for this opportunity to serve him in this way. I know that if I may be able to serve his servants, even with a little amount, that I'm doing this to him. Day by day my faith grows supernaturally. I began to focus more on the Lord, and became active with the online Bible study. I also had a consistent conversation with the pastor, and used to ask him questions, and he never hesitated to answer me and explain to me everything that I wanted to understand, and his name is pastor Joven Platilla. I praise God for giving me his servant that led me to love him above all else. The message that he gave me awakened me and empowered me, so that I now am busy sharing it with others. I was like a dried branch before, but by the mercies of God now I am a fruitful branch bearing much fruit for his glory, and this truth was confirmed to me by the Lord in a dream that I had twice. I saw in that dream a fruitful tree that was filled with fruits, and the Lord told me that the tree was none other than I. When I decided to listen to his voice, he made me fruitful. I praise God for giving me this opportunity to testify of his glory. To Jesus be the highest praise, amen.

(Note from pastor Joven:

As I was seeing the fruit that the Lord provided for us as a result of our obedience, I was greatly amazed, and was full of praise to his holy name.   I remember how the Lord showed us this in dreams, visions, even in a prophecy, and now these have become a reality. Hallelujah!)

Brother Raymond Esorio (Tayabas Quezon)

For a time, I used to meet religious people from different sects and denominations. They used to share to me their own beliefs about God, and I entertained them, yet none of them could persuade me to join them. I am a kind of "to see is to believe" person. Deep inside of me I knew that there is right path that I needed to take so as to see heaven. I was seeking, and at those times there were strange experiences that I often had that made me to look for an answer. I sometimes saw spirits, and even had some ideas popping up in my head about the future, like the car that can be run through a magnetic field. It can run even without gas.   I also had ideas about a plane that can fly without gas, and so on. I only was able to share this with my trusted friends, since not all have the desire to know such things. My encounter that led me to believe in Jesus as Lord and Savior happened when my sister-in-law, Rizalie, a leader of their church, brought their pastor to our place to share the gospel there. I met pastor Joven, and there was a thing that happened to me that time that made me to regard him differently from other religious people that visited me. My palms were sweating. The first time that I experienced this was when I met a mysterious man that told me to seek the truth, and after that he was gone. Pastor Joven silenced my confused mind by sharing with me the knowledge of the future that is in the Bible. I was amazed that what he shared to me has a connection to the things that pop up in my mind. I said, "This is an answer." Time went by, and they continued to visit our family once a month so as to share the gospel. Even after this, I still am longing for something - something deeper in the spirit. One of my breakthroughs happened when we visited them in July 2018, and during those days the Lord convicted me to lay down all that hinders me, to experience his power. I also had a connection to dark power that often made me into a different person for a time - like gaining supernatural strength so as to lift a huge and heavy stone, etc. Some said I have a spirit guide in me. My family also had a connection to occultism. I decided to let go of all of them, and then this made me to see what I was looking for, the things of heaven! During those prayer times that I had with the Lord, he showed me a vision of wonderful things that are made of gold, of people wearing white clothes, and even a great structure that I believe was not a simple house, but a huge palace only good for a king! I saw a beautiful clear and blue sea, as clear as crystal, and more. Hallelujah! This is what I'm looking for; thank you Jesus!

(Note from pastor Joven:

Brother Raymond's breakthrough happened when he decided to trust God with everything. At that time, he was struggling with the oppression that his family was experiencing from their neighbor. This neighbor built a piggery beside them, just ten meters away from them, with twenty to forty pigs! The air was being polluted, and they filed a complaint about this to their barangay, yet because of money, the officials closed their ears to the cry of almost twenty families in that place about this piggery polluting their air. The children got sick, and Raymond wasn't able to work for days, since even he was greatly affected because of the contaminated air and water. He even was tempted by demons to use force so as to remove the piggery from that neighborhood, but the Lord appeased him with his peace. The Lord promised to protect them and to act against that piggery in a matter of time; they only had to wait. As I observe the situation, it was as if God was using the situation to humble Raymond, and to teach him to trust only in him. Now, he dedicates himself to study the word of God and is determined to grow in the knowledge of him.)

Sister Nilay (Tayabas Quezon)

We came from a Roman Catholic belief, and used to be spiritually dry for years, even after becoming religious. God made a way for me to know his word by one of my relatives, and we became Christians. We used to attend our former church here at Tayabas, and serve God faithfully in that fellowship. Even after having a new direction from the Lord, I again little by little experienced spiritual dryness, and hunger and thirst for God. I longed for something more than attending church. More than singing, more than seeing people. I wanted spiritual breakthrough. One day I had a dream. In my dream I saw a servant of God powerfully preaching the word of God! This kind of message was what I was looking for, and this awakened me from the inside! Days, weeks, months, and even years passed by, and I almost forgot the dream; yet God didn't forget it. The Lord appointed a day for this dream that he gave to come to pass. In one of our night gatherings at the church, we learned that there would be visitors - a pastor with his leaders to minister to us. We held a revival night, and part of that video was uploaded by pastor Joven, though many doubted, maligned, and even falsely accused him of being a servant of Satan, and doing wrong, unbiblical, things. But I will tell you, since I was there, God was mightily moving that night! Also, that night was the fulfillment of the dream he gave me years ago. When we saw pastor Joven's team, they all looked like young people, and the young pastor didn't look like a pastor; he looked just like one of our youth leaders in the church. Yet when he began to preach the gospel, we were astounded by the power of conviction that God laid on us! We were all shaken to the core of our spirits. The message lasted more than an hour, and we all were amazed at the anointing that God had given to this young pastor.

Suddenly God impressed to me that he is the man that he showed me in a dream - the man that would preach the message that I was looking for. After the message, we had a prayer for baptism of the Holy Spirit and deliverance, and all the young people received the power of God and got delivered from demonic oppressions. That night was a significant night of spiritual breakthrough for us. God blessed us with the gift of tongues, visions, and even the holy fire. Even my children were blessed by God's power; hallelujah! After this the Lord revealed to us that he wanted us to get out of the church we were in, since the leader/pastor wasn't willing to get out of the old system that was taught to him, that had made the church spiritually dry for years. One of the youth leaders that went out with us from that church received a vision of Jesus standing outside the door of that church, and he was knocking! The old man-made system of the church pushes Jesus out of his church! How sad. In obedience to God's word, we got out of that church, and were persecuted by those that stayed, and we managed to little by little begin our new journey with the Lord, having our hearts filled with hope and power from the Lord. I really praise God for what he did to us and is continuing to do to our brethren and family.

Brother Daniel

John 3:16: *For God so loved the world, that he gave his only begotten Son, that whosoever believeth in him should not perish, but have everlasting life.*

I am Daniel Bacalso, 37 years old, and once was lost and was having a difficult life due to a broken family. My parents were separated from each other when I was three years old. It happened because my father was a drunkard, and he had vices, so our mom (they had just two children) decided to leave him. That separation made our life difficult. It's not good for children to have a broken family, and I later found out that our mom once planned to commit suicide. She only forgot about it when her sister preached to her about hell, and later on she and us children were invited to go to their church. My younger brother Dennis and I used to attend Sunday school in the church at our early age, yet I didn't know (had no personal encounter) with the Lord during that time. I only knew him through the stories taught to us, but I hadn't encountered him yet. It was when I was in my first year of high school that I had a personal encounter with the Lord. My brother was outside during that time, and my mom went to her work, and I was in our room alone, praying. I began praying differently than I used to before (with my mind only), and I began recognizing God in my heart, and I heard myself confessing all my sins before God, while tears flowed down on my cheeks. I repented for all of my sins, and decided to surrender my life to Jesus, asking for his forgiveness. Then suddenly I experienced this wonderful peace that I couldn't explain. This peace made me feel secure and complete. I experienced God's forgiveness and acceptance, as if he was embracing me at that time. The experience and the feeling were real, although I was physically alone in the room. I knew this was not just a hallucination - not just something that came from my own emotion, but was something real! This was God embracing me like a father embraces his lost son. As children, we lived our childhood without our father beside us, and were not even able to see his face or hear his voice, and not even receive his embrace. But when God embraced me, I know it was real, and I know that it was him! Jesus said, "My sheep hear my voice, and I know them." This knowing, I believe, was what I experienced when I surrendered my life to him. I felt his forgiveness, and I forgave all people that sinned against me. This was the beginning of Jesus choosing me to be his disciple. For now, I continue serving the Lord as one of the servants at Christ the Living Word Fire Ministry, and I am blessed being here. To God be all the glory!

(Note from pastor Joven:

Brother Daniel was the Lord's instrument to bring me into the fellowship. He first invited me to attend their small church, and after months, we decided to transfer from Antipolo to Laguna. We attended a full gospel church together, and learned together, until the Lord directed us to have an independent ministry (Christ the Living Word Fire Ministry), and I became the lead pastor, and he is one of our leaders. The Lord be glorified in our lives. Amen.)

Testimonies from our foreign brethren (live streaming viewers)

Pastor Jerikiah Hunter (Grace Based Church, Killeen Texas)

I met Pastor Joven through social media outlets. He was preaching the word of God and I was blessed by his message and passion for Jesus Christ. God put it into my heart to sow into his ministry. God is so moving in this ministry that revival is breaking out. I am truly blessed to know brother Joven. Blessings. Ephesians 3:20.

Cheryl Fricke

Love your ministry, because I know you are speaking and living for God - a true man of God. I pray, Father, that this book be an instrument for your glory. Millions will read it and receive the new life of your Holy Spirit. Amen.

The end

9 780999 587348